THE WORLD OF MUSIC

English and American Folk Music

THE
WORLD OF MUSIC

English and American Folk Music

RICHARD CARLIN

Facts On File Publications
New York, New York ● Oxford, England

Library of Congress Cataloging-in-Publication Data
Carlin, Richard.
  English and american folk music

  (The World of music ; vol. 2)
  Includes bibliographies and index.
  Summary: Defines folk music and traces its history and
development in Great Britain and the United States.
  1. Folk music—United States—History and criticism—
Juvenile literature. 2. Folk music—Great Britain—
History and criticism—Juvenile literature. [1. Folk
music—United States—History and criticism. 2. Folk
music—Great Britain—History and criticism] I. Title.
II. Series: World of music (New York, N.Y.) ; v. 2.
ML3545.C29   1986   784.4'941   86-19875
ISBN 0-8160-1381-0

Printed in the United States of America

10 9 8 7 6 5 4 3 2 1

Cover photo by McIntyre Photographers
Design and Production by Backes Graphic Productions

Contents

Preface

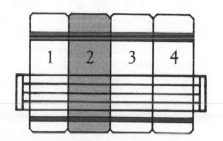

The World of Music is a series of books designed to introduce you to the different types of music found throughout the world. Each volume stands on its own as a basic introduction to a specific type of music; taken all together, the series will give a rich overview of man's musical achievements, and we hope will inspire your own music making and listening.

This volume describes the rich heritage of folk music found in the British Isles and the United States. It has been particularly meaningful for me to write this book, because I have been a folk musician and "folklorist" (a person who studies and records traditional folk music) since I was 17 years old.

Actually, my introduction to folk music came much earlier. My parents were fans of folk music in the 1930s and 1940s, when Pete Seeger, Woody Guthrie, and Leadbelly were first performing for city audiences. There were many old 78 records in my house of these performers which I listened to while I was growing up. One of the first records my parents bought for me was Pete Seeger's *Birds, Beasts, and Bigger Fishes,* a record of traditional American children's songs.

My older brother was an avid fan of all types of music and often played blues, early jazz, country, and folk records. Being much younger, I was not often invited in to listen to these records with him, so I surreptitiously listened through the wall of my bedroom. When I was 13 years old, instead of listening to Top 40 records, I was already a fan of such esoteric figures as Blind Lemon Jefferson.

When I was 15, I heard a folk performer playing the English concertina, a traditional folk instrument from Great Britain that resembles a small accordion. I soon owned a concertina, and was learning to play. When I was 17, I applied for and received a grant from the National Endowment for the Humanities in Washington, D.C. to record traditional concertina players in England. I was soon travelling abroad and the tapes that I made were eventually released as an album on Folkways records.

I continued to play folk music and to record traditional musicians at college. A group of Irish musicians living in Cleveland became close friends, and I was happy to be able to record three albums of their music. At the same time, I wrote an instruction book for the concertina, and began collecting traditional dance tunes which were later issued in one large book.

Why am I telling you my life story? I want you to realize that folk music is something that is still very much alive. Many of you probably have never heard the musicians in this book, either on record or in concert. You probably feel that the closest you'll ever come to "playing" music is when you "play" the radio or record player. I hope this book serves as an inspiration to you to become a musician. You don't have to play folk music, as I do; you should choose the music that you enjoy.

This book is only a starting point in your study of folk music. I have included select lists of records and books at the end of each chapter that can broaden your knowledge of different aspects of the music that we'll be discussing here. Many of the records have excellent liner notes or even come with small booklets, which often give more complete information about the music than some of the books that I mention. Most of these records and books come from small, specialized companies; be sure to ask your librarian where you can find them.

If you haven't studied music before, you probably will want to read the first volume in this series, *Man's Earliest Music*. The first half of that book gives a thorough introduction to music theory. Although you don't have to read that introduction in order to understand the discussion of folk music here, it certainly would help. The second half of that book describes four different musical cultures, the Aborigines of Australia, the peoples of the Pacific Islands, the African Pygmies, and the American Indians.

In the future, we are planning to produce more volumes to describe all aspects of music. The following volumes will be published shortly.

European Classical Music, 1600–1850: All of the major classical composers, the development of opera, music for strings, orchestral music, church music, music notation, and many other areas.

Rock and Roll: The birth of rock in country and city blues, black performers of the late 1940s and 1950s, rockabilly (country rock 'n' roll), and many major performers and musical trends, such as Elvis Presley, Buddy Holly, Little Richard, Chuck Berry, the girl groups of the early '60s, the Beatles and the British invasion, psychedelic rock, heavy metal, soul, Michael Jackson, disco, and rap.

Richard Carlin

Introduction to folk music

In this chapter, we'll introduce some of the basic concepts of folk music. First, what do we mean when we call something "folk music"? We'll examine how folk music is passed from person to person, across the generations. How does this method of transmitting folk song change it? We'll look at three examples of related folk songs, examining the structure of the lyrics and music. Finally, we'll compare folk music with classical and popular music, and discuss how folk music has survived in the modern world.

Who Are These Folk?

Developing a good definition of folk music involves deciding who are the "folk."

Folk in its broadest sense includes everyone who is a member of a particular nationality or ethnic group. Thus, the music of Bach is just as much a part of German folk music as a local German beer-drinking song. Although this definition is useful, it probably is too broad; all of a culture's music would have to be included in it.

The definition of "folk" as being members of a single cultural group becomes tricky when we look at some examples. Black American folk music is often studied as a part of what is called "Afro-American music." This includes not only folk music but blues, jazz, classical music composed by Blacks, and also pop forms, including disco, Motown, and rap. Black folk music has itself had a great influence on white folk, pop, jazz, and classical musics. We end up with a definition of "Black folk music" that seems to include just about everything.

Some people think the "folk" are the rural poor, such as farmers and people who labor on the land. This comes from an idea de-

1

veloped about 200 years ago among folklorists that the people who work the land in a country are the true "folk." They're the working class who sing songs about the changing seasons, and songs related to the work of growing and harvesting food and raising dairy animals and animals for the slaughter.

This definition would certainly eliminate quite a number of "folk." What about the working folk who work in factories? Don't they have their own songs? How about the owners of the factories and farms? How about college students, or for that matter, high school and elementary school students? They have their own songs, too. Aren't these groups also "folks"?

The answer is obviously yes. In order to better understand what is folk music, let's look at a more precise definition.

One Definition of Folk Music

In the early 1950s, the International Folk Music Council came up with a definition of folk music that set the framework for studying the wealth of music created by folk all across the globe. They identified three crucial factors in folk music that places it apart from other forms of musical expression: *continuity*, *variation*, and *selection*.

Continuity means that a song has been known for many generations, and is sung more or less in the same way. *Variation* means that, as each singer learns the song, he or she adds personal changes to the words, melody, or rhythm. A particular singer may forget a verse, or add a new verse, or put two songs together, or take one set of words and set it to a different melody. Although a song continues to be sung over the years (continuity), it changes as it passes through the hands of different singers (variation).

The third factor, *selection*, indicates that a community of people will select the songs that they choose to pass on to the next generation. This doesn't occur through a thought-out or conscious process of saying "Well, this song seems to be a good one, let's pass it along," but rather, as songs become more popular, more singers will sing them, and these songs will survive.

The International Folk Music Council said that popular, composed music could also be considered folk music, as long as it meets the three criteria of being sung by many singers over many generations (continuity), changed by the singers (variation), and selected by the community (selection).

Today's popular music could very well be tomorrow's folk music. Let's take one example: Bob Dylan's 1960s protest song, "Blowin' in the Wind," is often called a folk song, even though we know who composed it and when it was composed. Even though the song is only a little over 20 years old, it already has changed as different singers have sung it. The melody, rhythm, and words have all been altered, even by Bob Dylan himself when he has made different recordings of the song and played it at many different concerts. Parody versions, with lyrics making fun of the original song or with lyrics addressing other social problems, have been written and sung.

Now, let's imagine the year 2100. It's possible that singers in that time will still be singing "Blowin' in the Wind." Of course, musical instruments will be different. The issues that were raised in the song will all have changed. If phonograph records and record players still survive, people will be able to hear Bob Dylan's original version. But probably the original record will only be available in special libraries, if it's available at all. It's more likely that there will be many different versions of "Blowin' in the Wind," all based on the original, but none the same. The song will then truly be a folk song.

Oral Transmission

When scholars talk about folk music, they often mention the words "oral transmission ." Simply put, oral transmission means that each musician learns a new song or tune by hearing it performed by another musician. There are no written scores, as there are in classical music.

Although oral transmission is the most important way that folk songs are spread, it can also lead to changes in the music. These changes can improve the song, by eliminating verses that aren't interesting, or shortening the story so that it is more easily sung. Or the changes can be bad, as some of the examples that follow will show.

The Game of Telephone

You've probably played the game telephone or password. In this game, a group of people gather in a circle or line. The first person whispers a word into the next person's ear. The next person then whispers the same word into the third person's ear, and so on and on. The last person then says the word aloud. Sometimes, it's the same word that the first person said; sometimes, the word has been changed by being passed from person to person. It could be a word that sounds similar, or a word with a similar meaning, or a totally different word, or even a meaningless sound. Why does this happen?

As the word is repeated from person to person, a number of things can happen that will result in it being changed. Imagine that one person in the line is hard of hearing. He or she could easily mishear what is being said. Or, maybe this person is simply bored with the game, and not listening too carefully. Again, he or she could misunderstand and pass along a different word. Maybe one person in the line never heard of the word that is being passed along, so he or she substitutes a different word. Or, maybe this person mispronounces the word, so that the next person thinks that it's a different word. These are just a few possibilities.

Now, imagine the game of password being played across many generations. Imagine that your great-great-great-grandfather whispered a word to his son. This son taught the word to his daughter, but by then the way that words were pronounced had changed. The daughter moves to a new country, and translates the word into a new language before teaching it to her daughter. This daughter misunderstands the word, and so teaches another word to her son. He moves to another country, and so on and on.

Imagine that each person is teaching a song, rather than a word, to the next person in line down through the generations. How would the melody, words, and meaning of the song change?

Changes that Occur in Oral Transmission

Roger Abrahams and George Foss have made a list of the changes that can occur to a song as it is passed along through oral transmission. These include:

1. Degenerative Causes
   a. Mishearing
   b. Forgetting
   c. Misunderstanding
2. Community Attitudes
3. Universalization and Localization

Most of the changes that we've already discussed as occurring in the game of password or telephone are degenerative changes. In other words, through some failure of understanding by the next person in line, the word is not passed along correctly. Abrahams and Foss list three types of degenerative changes: mishearing, forgetting, and misunderstanding.

Forgetting may be the most complicated item in this list. A person might forget the entire text and melody of a song that really isn't interesting to him or her. Or, a singer might remember a single verse that stands out from the rest, because of the beauty of the lyrics, the content or message that the words of that particular verse are expressing, or simply because it was the last verse that was sung. A singer might remember a melody, but forget all (or some) of the words. There have been cases of individual singers taking verses from several different songs and stringing them together into a new song. Sometimes a person makes up new verses to fill out a song, when she or he can only remember one or two of the original verses.

Community attitudes are a second important factor in the survival of a song. For example, some Southern ballad singers refuse to sing "The House Carpenter," a ballad that tells the story of a woman abandoning her newborn baby in order to run away with her lover. In the end, both the heroine and her lover are drowned, apparently as punishment for their crimes. Almeda Riddle, an Ozark mountain singer, loves to sing the song, but felt uncomfortable hearing it as a child, because of the way the heroine acts:

> I thought that was a terrible thing, this mother leaving that baby. That was the thing that struck me the worst. . . . And when she drowned, I remembered getting great satisfaction out of the thought that she got her just desserts.

Other singers refuse to sing this ballad, because they feel the actions of the heroine are "immoral."

Universalization and localization refer to two different forces that tend to change songs. A song that tells the story of an event in Ohio may only appeal to Ohio residents. A singer who sings the song in New York may change the names of the towns and people in the song to make it more appealing to a New York

Spanish American musicians at a fiesta. Taos, New Mexico. PHOTOGRAPH: Russell Lee. Reproduction from the Collections of the Library of Congress.

audience. He or she is *localizing* the song. *Universalization* is the opposite of localization. In this case, instead of giving local names to characters or towns, the singer will substitute general (generic) names. A song about Joe Smith from Anytown, U.S.A. would be an example of the use of generic or standard names.

A fourth method of oral change is a singer choosing deliberately to make changes in a song. Sometimes, a singer simply will not like the melody or the words of a particular song, and so will change them. For example, a song that features physical violence might be edited by parents when they sing it to their children. These same children might enjoy singing only the blood-and-guts verses among themselves.

More often, this process of deliberately changing a song is a creative one. A singer may have a personal style, and so will choose specific types of melodies that highlight this style. For example, a singer who can imitate animal sounds, and is well known for this capability, might insert verses into a song that call for these sounds, such as the whistling of birds, the barking of dogs, or the mooing of cows. Singers who are less talented in this area will delete the verses that call for these sounds.

The Shaping of Songs through Oral Transmission

To understand how oral transmission works, let's look at a few examples from British and American folk music. We'll begin by looking at how the words to songs are shaped by being learned orally, and then briefly discuss how melodies travel from song to song.

Compression and Repetition

Compression and repetition are the most common changes that occur to songs through oral transmission. *Compression* means that the story that is told in a song is compressed or made shorter. *Repetition* means that key phrases, verses, or even sections of a song are repeated over and over again. Let's look at one example, the English ballad "The Prickelly Bush," also known as "The Maid Freed from the Gallows" (Child #95). * This version is from Julia Scaddon, recorded in the 1950s by Peter Kennedy in the English town of Chideock in Dorsetshire. It can be heard on Topic Records *The Child Ballads I,* catalogue number 160.

---

*The Child numbers for ballads were assigned by Francis James Child in his 5-volume collection of traditional songs (see Chapter 2).

Prickelly Bush

1 O hangman, hold my hand,
   And hold it for a while,
   I think I see my own mother dear,
   Coming o'er yonder stile.

2 Oh, have you brought me gold,
   Or can you set me free?
   Or are you come to see me hang
   All on the gallows tree?

3 No, I've not brought you gold,
   Nor I can't set you free,
   For I have come to see you hang.
   All on the gallows tree.

4 O the prickelly bush
   That pricks my heart from sore,
   If I ever get out of the prickelly bush,
   I'll never get in it no more.

5–8 —Father

9–12 —Brother

13–16 —Sister

17 O hangman, hold my hand,
   And hold it for a while,
   I think I see my own sweetheart
   Comin' o'er yonder stile.

18 Oh, have you brought me gold!
   Or can you set me free?
   Or are you come to see me hang
   All on the gallows tree?

19 Yes, I have brought you gold,
   And I can set you free.
   But I'm not come to see you hanged
   All on the gallows tree.

20 Oh, the prickelly bush
   That pricks my heart from sore,
   Now that I'm out of the prickelly bush.
   I'll never get in it no more.

This ballad offers an excellent example of how compression and repetition work. The story has obviously been shortened. We don't know why the young girl is waiting to be hanged; what crime did she commit? Who is this girl, a rich lady, the daughter of a nobleman, a milkmaid? From this version of the song, we can't tell; by looking at other versions that have been collected in England, we know that the girl was a servant who stole something from her employer, usually a gold ring or ball. But, in most versions, the actual crime is not described. Why might this be so?

The focus of the song is on the maid's predicament. She's waiting to die, and her parents and siblings can't help her. It doesn't matter why they can't help her, although in some versions they are so mean that they want to see her die, while in other versions they are simply unable to offer help. The important thing is that no one can help; that is, until her lover arrives. He is the only one who can save her from death. When you think about it, this is quite a romantic situation; in the nick of time, her sweetheart arrives with the gold needed to pay to have her freed from the gallows.

Through compression, the story has been shortened to focus on this one important event. Roger Abrahams and George Foss call this the "emotional core" of the song. In this example, as we have already said, it doesn't matter how the girl got into trouble or even why no one can help her; the key thing is that she is in trouble, and only her sweetheart can help. The song focuses on this most dramatic aspect of the story, and all the rest is left out.

You can clearly see how repetition is at work in this song. It only consists of four verses. As each new person comes to the gallows, their name is substituted in the first verse:

"I think I see my mother dear . . ."
"I think I see my father dear . . ."
"I think I see my own sweetheart . . ."

Otherwise, the verses are unchanged, until the 19th and 20th verses, when the sweetheart says he does have the gold and can set her free. The song could be made longer or shorter simply by adding or deleting relatives (uncles, aunts, and so on).

You might think that the fourth verse (beginning "Oh the prickelly bush . . .") might be left out by singers over the years. After all, the words don't seem to have any direct connection to the maid's predicament. In fact, this verse serves as a kind of chorus; in some situations, the singer might be joined by the listeners in singing this verse as it occurs throughout the song. And even though you might not be able to say exactly what it means, the prickelly bush could be a symbol for the maid's difficult dilemma. Most important, the verse is fun to sing, and I think this is one reason it has survived.

Formula and Commonplace

Abrahams and Foss point out many other ways that the lyrics of folksongs are shaped by oral tradition. Two other important elements in folksong are *formula* and *commonplace*.

A *formula* is a standard way of starting or ending a song. This can consist of a single line; for example, many ballads begin with the line "One morning, one morning, one morning in May." This helps set the stage for the action that will follow. Sometimes, a formula can consist of one or more verses that come at the end of a song. Often, at the end of a particularly tragic ballad, the hero or heroine will call on his or her parents to:

Go dig my grave, both wide and deep,
Place a marble slab at my head and feet.
In the middle of my grave place a turtle dove
To show the world, I died for love.

This ending is found in ballads in both Britain and America.

Commonplace refers to any phrase or description that occurs in many different ballads. This commonplaces become the building blocks for creating a description of a character or an event. For example, horses are usually described as "milk-white steeds" or "dapple greys." When the hero of a ballad is tired, he expresses his fatigue by saying "I'm weary and fain would lie down." Women are described as having "lily-white hands"; when a hero is stabbed, his "heart's blood will flow"; and so on.

Versions and Variants

Songs in the oral tradition don't exist in a single form. They change as different singers give them their own personal twist. Here are two other versions of "The Maid Freed From the Gallows," one from Frank Proffitt (1913–1965), a white banjo player from North Carolina, and the other from Huddie Ledbetter (1885–1949), better known as Leadbelly, a black guitarist from Louisiana.

We might begin by noticing that each song has a different title and a different melody, even though we can recognize that all three are versions of the same song. In fact, we could print here a hundred or more versions of this song, all remarkably similar in lyrics, with a wide range of melodies (some similar, some very different).

Hold Up Your Hand

Hold up your hand, Old Joshuway, she said,
Wait a while and see,
I thought I see my dear old father,
Come a-crossing over the sea.

Do you have any money for me?
Gold to pay my fee?
I've just stole a silvery cup
And hangeth I'm a-goin to be.

I don't have no money for you,
Or gold to pay your fee.
I've just come to see you hanged,
On yonders gallows tree.

(Mother . . .)

(True love . . .)

Yes, I have some money for you,
And gold for to pay your fee
I've just come to save your neck
From yonders gallows tree.

(Recorded by Sandy Paton in September 1961, words and music in B.H.
Bronson, *The Singing Tradition of the Child Ballads*, Princeton, N.J.: Princeton
University Press, 1976.)

Gallows Pole

*The guitar fills are melody lines played on the guitar
(I haven't notated them here).

Father, did you bring me the silver,
Father, did you bring me the gold?
What did you bring me dear father
To keep me from the gallow's pole?
Lord, I brought it, Lord, I thought it,
You would bring me to keep from the gallow's pole.

Son, I brought you some silver,
Son, I brought you some gold,
Son, I brought you some everything
To keep from the gallow's pole
Lord . . . I brought it . . . Lord . . . I thought it . . .
You would bring me to keep from the gallow's pole.

[Spoken: Here comes his mother]

Mother . . .

[Spoken: She brought it too]

Son, I brought you some silver . . .

[Spoken: Now, here comes the so-called friend. So-called friend, it's the best
place he wants to see you in, not out. When you're out, you shake a so-called
friend's hand, you can't tell what it's all about. But when you get in, that's
the place the so-called friend wants to see you in. And you know what he
asked the so-called friend;]

Friend, did you bring me the silver,
Friend, did you bring me the gold,
What did you bring me my dear friend,
To keep me from the gallow's pole.
What did you . . . bring me . . . What did you . . . bring me
Bring me to keep from the gallow's pole.

I never brought you no silver,
I never brought you no gold,
I just come by to see you
Hung up on the gallow's pole.
Lord . . . I brought it . . . Lord . . . I thought it
See you hung up on the gallow's pole.

(From Leadbelly, *Shout On!* Folkways Records #31030. Recorded by Frederic
Ramsey Jr. in October, 1948)

The lyrics of the version from North Carolina are similar to the
one from England. The singer mixes both old words ("hangeth")
that probably come from a version of the song as it was sung some
centuries ago, and new words ("a-goin") that show the singers
Southern-mountain heritage.

Leadbelly's version is quite different. Here, the mother and father
come to help the son, and the "so-called friend" is the one who
wants to see him die. The spoken comments between the verses,
particularly before the last two verses, help drive home this message
to the listener.

Of course, the main difference among these three versions is
how they sound. Julia Scaddon sings her version without accompaniment, and so doesn't have to keep as closely to the beat as the
other two singers. Also, she emphasizes certain words in the song,
particularly the words that express sorrow (for example, she'll start
each chorus by holding the word "oh" to emphasize the maid's
predicament). Frank Proffitt sings in a low-keyed style, very
smoothly and cleanly. His banjo accompaniment is simple and
restrained. Leadbelly sings very emotionally. The guitar part plays
an important role in the song, echoing and reinforcing the melody.
Also, he emphasizes the offbeat in his accompaniment, giving a
syncopated, jazzy sound to the melody.

You could hardly imagine three more different arrangements. In
fact, it's hard to believe that this song, which is at least five

centuries old in one form or another, could appeal to three so very different people. The fact that it has survived is one testimony to the power of oral transmission.

Tunes in the Oral Tradition

The tunes of songs travel across space (from region to region) and time (from generation to generation). Although there are thousands of traditional tunes, some have become so popular that they will be used to accompany many different sets of words. Sometimes a singer will take a tune that he or she likes, and decide to use it for a ballad that was learned with a different tune. Sometimes, the original tune for a ballad is lost over time, and a new one is substituted. For whatever reason, tunes are swapped from singer to singer and from the past to the present.

Tunes are also shaped by singers. Sometimes, a note will fall out of the range of a particular singer; this note will be changed. Or, one part of a melody might not appeal to a singer, so it will be altered. Sometimes, the change happens simply through the process of singing, without any conscious decision to make the change. Just as words are unconsciously shaped, melodies too are changed from one singer to the next.

High Culture, Pop Culture, and Folk Culture

In studying folk music, it is interesting to compare it with two other musical forms: classical music and popular music. Folk music is an example of what anthropologists call "folk culture"; classical music is part of "high culture"; popular music is part of "pop culture." What do these three distinctions mean?

Before civilizations, there were no separate classes. With the growth of societies came different levels for different people: kings were more powerful than noblemen who, in turn, had more power than the common folk, who in turn were higher up the ladder than slaves or servants. Each level in society developed its own culture; the music written for kings was never performed for commoners, while it's unlikely that a king would ever have heard the harvest songs, beer-drinking ballads, and love songs of the ordinary folk.

High culture is the name given to the music and art directed to the highest levels of society. Classical music, for example, was originally written to be heard only by kings and noblemen. In fact, many of these noblemen commissioned specific works or even supported single composers for their entire lifetimes. The composer's job was to write music to please his listeners. Sometimes this involved writing wedding music, sometimes music to accompany a funeral.

The music of the upper classes was not learned through oral transmission. The composer hired other musicians to perform his music, and, to protect his music from being performed without his permission, he wrote it down. The nobleman who commissioned the work wanted something that was unique, because, after all, he was paying to get something unusual and beautiful, not just a common melody. The finished product would be performed for a small handful of friends of the nobleman, perhaps only in a single performance.

Folk music, on the other hand, is not individually composed. As we have already pointed out, generations of singers and musicians change the music to suit their needs. The music that each musician performs is not unique to him or her; it is something that is known by an entire culture. An individual musician might create a unique version of a song, but more often his or her version shares at least some elements with the version known and sung for hundreds of years. The song would be performed freely for anyone who wanted to listen, and would be widely known by all people in a culture.

This split between high culture and folk culture occurred fairly recently in European history, about 500 or so years ago. More recently, a third form of culture has developed, called pop culture. Pop culture is a product of the mass-market age, when music, art, and literature have been sold directly to consumers. Like classical or high culture, pop music is composed by an individual composer, and is written down and copyrighted so no one else can claim to be the author. But, like folk music, it is designed to appeal to a large audience.

The split between folk and high culture is less significant than it might first appear. High culture has always had an impact on folk culture; wandering minstrels, who performed at court, also made extra money by travelling to village fairs, bringing court songs to the masses. Many folk songs can be traced back to individual composers who worked in the courts. On the other hand, folk melodies have inspired classical composers. Beethoven, Bach, and Mozart all borrowed melodies from their native folk cultures.

The Survival of Folk Music

Roger Abrahams and George Foss point out two important elements that help a song survive in oral transmission. The song must be *memorable*, that is, the story must have an impact on the singer and his or her audience, and the song must be *easy to remember*, that is, it can't be so complicated that it's impossible for even the most talented singers to keep the melody and words in mind.

We've already examined some of the elements that make a song both memorable and easy to remember. We can only guess why some songs have become popular throughout the Western world, while others survive only in the hands of a few isolated singers. There is no way this process can be controlled; we may like certain songs better than others, but this doesn't guarantee that they will survive.

Today, the oral tradition continues, even though it takes new forms. For example, when you sit down and play your favorite rock 'n' roll record over and over until you learn the words, you're learning the song by hearing it being played. You aren't learning it from the actual musician; the phonograph record takes his or her place.

Although you may try to exactly duplicate what you hear, you may misunderstand a word, or be unable to reach a certain note. In this way, you'll change the song from what the performer originally created to something new. This is all part of the oral tradition/folk process. Learning from records, tape recordings, videocassettes, or from television performances is part of the new oral tradition.

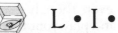

R•E•A•D

Abrahams, Roger and George Foss, *Anglo-American Folksong Style*. Englewood Cliffs, NJ: Prentice-Hall, 1968.

Abrahams, Roger and George Foss, Eds., *A Singer and Her Songs: Almeda Riddle's Book of Ballads*. Baton Rouge, LA: Louisiana State University Press, 1970.

Bronson, B.H. *The Singing Tradition of the Child Ballads*. Princeton, NJ: Princeton University Press, 1976.

Nettl, Bruno, *An Introduction to Folk Music in the United States*. Detroit, MI: Wayne State University Press, 1972.

Nettl, Bruno, *Folk and Traditional Music of the Western Continents* (2nd edition). Englewood Cliffs, NJ: Prentice-Hall, 1973.

Sandberg, Larry and Dick Weissman, *The Folk Music Sourcebook*. New York: Alfred A. Knopf, 1976.

L•I•S•T•E•N

Leadbelly, *Shout On!* Folkways FTS 31030.

Proffitt, Frank, *Vols. 1 and 2*. Folk Legacy 1, 36.

Scaddon, Julia, *The Child Ballads 1*. Topic 160.

2

Vocal and instrumental music forms

In this chapter, we'll look briefly at a little music theory in order to explain how British and American folk music is structured. First, we'll look at vocal music, examining the types of songs that have been created, how these songs are structured, and some aspects of melody (scale) and rhythm. Then, we'll take a quick look at the forms of dance music, how they evolved, and how they are structured.

Types of Vocal Music

The wealth of British and American folk songs can be divided into two very large categories: Songs that tell a story (Narrative songs), and Songs that express a mood (Lyrical songs). Let's take a close look at each category.

Narrative Songs

Narrative songs tell a story, which could be the history of a particular event, such as a fire, flood, or famous battle, or the story of an individual's life, or the story of a society and how it grew. There are two main types of narrative songs: Epic songs and ballads.

Epics are usually very long songs. They describe the heroic exploits of a famous warrior. All of the event of a hero's life will be recounted, moving from youth to old age. For this reason, an epic may appear to ramble from one place to another and from one time period to another, with the only connection among the events being the personality of the hero. Epics are most commonly found in Mideastern cultures, where singers will spend several evenings singing of the deeds of a local hero. The *Iliad* and the *Odyssey* by Homer are poems that were probably originally sung, and represented at least fragments of great Greek epics. In Great Britain, epics are still sung that recount the deeds of the mythical Gaelic kings Fionn and his son Ossian, but only a handful of singers know these songs. Often, the Ossian songs that have been collected include only a few verses, and so really aren't true epics.

Ballads are far more common than epics in Great Britain and America. Ballads are songs that tell a story, just like epics, but unlike the epic, a ballad focuses on a single event. The word "ballad" literally means a dance song, and has the same root as the word "ballet." Some scholars believe that at one time ballads were sung to accompany dances; many ballads include repeated refrains (or one-line choruses) that may have been sung by a group of dancers in response to the verse of the song (sung by a dance leader). Ballads usually feature a strong, regular rhythm, as opposed to epics which often are rhythmically freer, another element linking them to the dance.

The ballads that have been collected in Britain and the United States can be divided into two broad groups: (1) the older traditional ballads; and (2) more recently composed ballads. The first category includes most of the songs that deal with topics such as the courtship of a king, or a battle with a magical demon, or the murderous relationships among family members. These songs can be traced back at least 500 years, and have been passed from singer to singer across the centuries.

The second category consists primarily of the so-called "broadside ballads." In the 17th through 19th centuries, many small print shops opened, and the ability to read (or *literacy*) spread from the middle to the lower classes. Broadsides were single sheets of paper, with the words to a newly composed ballad printed on the front. These ballads often recounted the "news of the day," and were set to well-known traditional melodies.

During the 18th century, scholars began to realize that ballads should be preserved. One of the most famous scholars lived in Boston in the 19th century. He was Harvard professor Francis James Child (1825–1896); his work in preserving folk ballads led to the publication of a five-volume work. The songs collected by Child are commonly called *Child ballads*, and are considered to be some of the greatest traditional songs.

Lyric Songs

Scholars have given the name "lyric songs" to a group of songs that express emotions or feelings, rather than tell a story. I've included in this category the wealth of nonnarrative vocal music found in Britain and American, including: 1. Love songs, 2. Work songs, 3. Protest songs, 4. Religious songs, 5. Fun and party songs, 6. Songs of the lifestages.

Love Songs

There are two types of love songs that are commonly found in the Anglo-American tradition. The first type includes songs that can be traced back to the court music of the Middle Ages. In these songs, the singer often pines for his beloved, but rarely, if ever, actually meets her. The loved one is the perfect woman, whose beauty is described in terms of commonplace phrases such as "rosey-red cheeks" and "milk-white skin." The lover often imagines himself being magically transported to his love, as in this verse from the American song "Pretty Saro":

I wish I were a small bird, had wings and could fly;
Right to my love's dwelling this night I'd draw nigh;
In her lily-white arms all night I would lie,
And out some small window next morning I'd fly.

Romantic love songs express longing, sadness, and unfulfilled desires. The second type of love song is far more common in folk music; this expresses love as a natural part of the everyday world. In these songs, the lover doesn't pine after his true love, but makes the best of every situation. If he's rejected, he's more than likely to say "there are more fish in the sea" than to feel sorry for himself. In these songs, love is not the inspiration for a dreamy feeling, but rather a part of the business of raising a family.

Work Songs and Protest Songs

Work songs are an entire family of songs sung to help pass the time while working, or to help keep a large work force working together by maintaining a steady beat. Work songs are associated with agriculture (growing crops, tending animals), manual labor (laying railroad tracks, coal mining, breaking up rocks), working at machines (operating large looms for spinning thread), or household chores (tending to the needs of young children).

Protest songs have been known as long as there have been divisions in society between the rich and the poor. The poor have expressed their frustrations with unfair laws, poor working conditions, sickness, and lack of freedom by writing songs. Every new

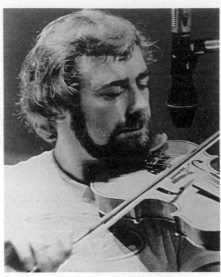

Shetland fiddler Aly Bain.
PHOTO COURTESY: Flying Fish Records.

generation has new concerns, and creates its own songs expressing these feelings.

Religious Songs

Religious songs can be broken into two categories: (1) folksongs associated with ancient rituals; and (2) hymns written and promoted by Christian, Protestant, and other modern religions. Folk religious rituals include such common practices as Christmas carolling (originally associated with the midwinter solstice, carolling was performed to ensure the return of warm weather in the spring), singing to inspire spirits (a common practice is singing songs to apple trees to help the apple spirits to create more and healthier fruit), special ritual songs associated with the different seasons of the years, and songs to cast or remove spells.

Many of these songs were sung as part of the ancient custom of wassailing. The word "wassail" literally means "good health"; strolling wassailers would sing songs to bring health from house to house. In this apple tree wassail, singers address the owner of the orchard, asking him to come down and let them into his house to get warm by the fire. Then, they sing a short verse addressed to the apple trees:

> Lily, white lily, oh lily, white pin,
> Please to come down and let us come in.
> How well you may bloom, how well you may bear,
> So we may have apples and cider next year.

Modern hymns in a Christian or Protestant hymnal come from a wide variety of sources. Some of these hymns are based on melodies from the classical composers. However, church musicians who have assembled the hymnals have recognized the popularity of folk melodies and have taken these melodies and adapted new words to them. One of the most popular examples is "Amazing Grace," a hymn set to an ancient folk tune that has been sung for hundreds of years, and has been performed by pop singers like Judy Collins.

Fun Songs and Songs of the Lifestages

Traditional folk music includes a wealth of songs that are sung merely for fun. Some of these songs include nonsense words that are fun to sing, often as a chorus. One subgroup is songs that tell outrageous lies; here's an example from the Shetland Islands tradition:

> When I was a little boy to London I did go,
> But now I've turned a roguish blade, my courage it will show.
> My feet was on the table, sir, my head was hanging down,
> And I jumped over Kingston's Hill, and never touched the ground,
> CHORUS: With my tooral laddy, whack fol laddy, tooral looral ling.
>
> I bought myself a little hen, and of her I took great care,
> I set her on a mussel shell and she hatched me out a hare
> The hare grew up a milk-white steed, about 18 inches high,
> And if anyone tell you a bigger story, you know it's a bloody lie.
> (CHORUS) . . .

Songs of lifestages are special songs sung to mark specific turning points in a person's life: when a young man or woman reaches puberty, marries, has his or her first child, or dies. Children's songs are an important subgroup within this category. There are songs that parents sing to children, either to teach them how to do something, or what not to do, or songs simply to amuse them. Then there are the songs children sing. Often, these will be silly songs, or songs that make fun of the foolish things that adults do.

The Structure of Vocal Music

Bruno Nettl, in his book *Folk and Traditional Music of the Western Continents,* has pointed out a unique feature of European folk music in general, and Anglo-American folk music in particular: songs have "a structure in which a tune with several lines is repeated several times, each time with different words." This structure is called a *strophe* or *stanza*, and it is one element that unites all European folk music, and classical and popular music as well.

Let's take an example from a popular ballad, "Barbara Allen."

Barbara Allen

O   down in Lon--don where   I was raised, down

where I got my learn-ing I fell in love with a

pret-ty lit-tle girl Her name was Bar-b'ry Al-len

1 O down in London where I was raised,
   Down where I got my learning,
   I fell in love with a pretty little girl,
   Her name was Barb'ry Allen.

2 He courted her for seven long years,
   She said she would not have him.
   Pretty William went home and took down sick,
   And sent for Barb'ry Allen.

3 He wrote her a letter on his deathbed,
   He wrote it slow and moving,
   Go take this to my pretty little love,
   And tell her I am dying.

   [Verses 4–5 omitted]

6 Do you remember last Saturday night,
   Down at your father's dwelling,
   You passed the drink to the ladies all around,
   And slighted Barb'ry Allen.

7 O yes, I remember last Saturday night,
   Down at your father's dwelling,
   I passed the drink to the ladies all around,
   But my heart to Barb'ry Allen.

8 As she walked down those long stair-steps,
   She heard some deathbells ringings,
   And every bell it seemed to say,
   Hard-hearted Barb'ry Allen.
   Hard-hearted Barb'ry Allen. *

9 As she walked down that shady grove
   She heard some birds a-singing,
   And every bird it seemed to say,
   Hard-hearted Barb'ry Allen.
   Hard-hearted Barb'ry Allen. *

   [verses 10–12 omitted]

13 O father, O father, go dig my grave,
   Go dig it deep and narrow;
   Sweet William died for me today,
   And I'll die for him tomorrow.

14 A rose grew up from William's grave,
   From Barbara Allen's a brier,
   They grew and they grew to the top of the church,
   Til they could grow no higher.

15 They grew and they grew to the top of the church
   Till they could grow no higher,
   And there they tied in a true love's knot
   And the rose wrapped around the brier.
   *In these verses, the last line of music and words is repeated once.

In this song, the second line and the fourth line rhyme. This structure could be described as A-B-C-B. Another common ballad structure is A-B-A-B, where the first and third lines rhyme, and the second and fourth lines rhyme.

The regular, repeated structure of the verses is complimented by the regular, repeated structure of the music. If you look for a moment at the music, you'll see that the melody can be broken into four parts, each phrase accompanying one line of text. Longer notes in the melody tend to come at the ends of a line of the verse, allowing the singer to pause for breath or to emphasize a key point in the narrative.

You might notice some more subtle elements of the structure of the song. The words "Barb'ry Allen," that often come at the end of a stanza, are almost a miniature chorus; you can imagine other people in the room joining in on these words. When the words "Barb'ry Allen" are not included at the end of a verse, words with a similar rhythm are substituted for them:

Bar---bry   Al---len
die to — mor--row
round the   bri--er
              and so on

You might also notice how sometimes an entire verse is repeated, with just a few small changes, as in the sixth and seventh verses where Barbara asks the young man if he remembers when he slighted her, and he responds that he does remember. Notice also how the last two lines of the 14th stanza are repeated at the beginning of the 15th stanza.

This version includes a formulaic ending (see Chapter 1). In this ending, the two lovers are buried, and from their graves spring a rose and a briar, which join together to form the "true-lover's knot." This same ending can be found in many ballads that tell the story of tragic love affairs.

Scale and Rhythm

I don't want to delve too deeply into music theory, but I would like to briefly describe some of the general characteristics of Anglo-American vocal music. For those of you unfamiliar with musical terms, you may wish to review Chapter 2 in the first book in this series, *Man's Earliest Music*.

European folk music scales tend to be *pentatonic*; that is, they feature five notes. In the version of Barbara Allen that we've just discussed, these five notes are G–B flat–C–D–F.

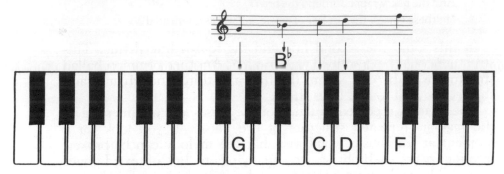

As you can see, these five notes are not right next to each other on the piano keyboard, so we call this type of scale a "gapped scale" (because there are gaps between the notes).

European scales commonly are based on *intervals* or gaps of major seconds and minor thirds. A *major second* is the space between two white keys on the piano, such as C to D. It is three steps up the scale (C–C#–D).

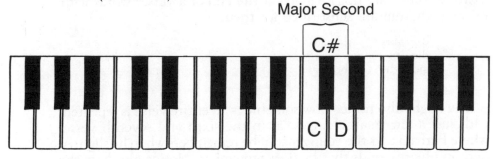

A *major third* is the gap between three white keys, such as C to E. A *minor third* is a half-step shorter, such as C to E flat. It is four steps up the scale (C–C#–D–D# or E flat).

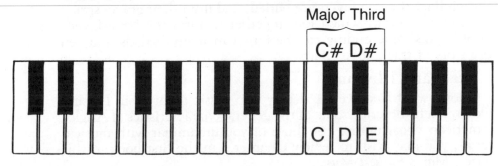

Let's look at the scale from Barbara Allen. G to B flat is a minor third; B flat to C is a major second (because there's no black note between B and C; look at the keyboard); C to D is a major second; and D to F is a minor third (D to F# is a major third: why?).

You may have noticed the regular rhythmic structure of Barbara Allen. Almost all Anglo-American folk songs, with the exception perhaps of epics and laments, adhere to a strict rhythm. These rhythms are usually based on two pulses per measure (duple rhythms) or three pulses per measure (triple rhythms). Most songs are *isometric*; that is, one rhythmic pulse is used throughout the song (the singer doesn't change from $\frac{2}{4}$ in one part of the song to $\frac{3}{4}$ in another).

Within this strict rhythm, there is some flexibility from singer to singer. A singer might pause on one note, or sing a line with an extra measure, or delete a measure from one line. These small changes don't change the overall feeling of a regular rhythm. Note in this version of "Barbara Allen" that the singer adds an extra line to the eighth and ninth verses.

Ornament

When we look at the notation of "Barbara Allen," it looks very much like a classical or popular song. The notes are the ordinary notes we find on a piano, and the rhythm appears regular. However, if we listen to a recording of a traditional singer, we may be surprised to hear the way that he or she sings this seemingly "ordinary" song. The way that a singer changes a song is called *ornament*.

An ornament is literally an extra grace note or grace notes that are attached to a primary note in a song, or a vocal glide up to a note, or bending a note to change its pitch, or singing with a quavering voice (*vibrato*), to name just a few possibilities. I am defining ornament to also include any variation in the way the singer performs a song.

Folk singers usually prefer a nasal, intense singing style to the relaxed, open-throat style heard in popular music. When you first hear a folk singer perform, you might think that he or she simply doesn't know the "right way" to sing. Actually, these performers choose to sing in this throaty style, sometimes purposely adding a raspy, cutting sound to their singing voice.

Traditional singers may also vary the attack or accent on an individual note. *Attack* refers to the volume and speed with which a singer performs a given note; *accent* indicates which notes stand out from the rest, due to sharp attack. A singer may accent the offbeats, creating what is known as *syncopation*. A singer may draw out certain notes, shorten others, and vary singing volume from a whisper to a scream.

It is impossible to generalize from culture to culture, or even from region to region. Singers from one area of Southern Appalachia, centered in Deep Gap, North Carolina, sing in a fairly relaxed style. Jean Ritchie (1922–   ), a famous folk singer you may have heard perform, comes from that area. Further south, you are more likely to hear the intense, nasal singing that is typical of folk performers. The important thing is to listen to every singer or musician with an open mind, and to remember that there are always exceptions to every rule.

Instrumental Music

Instrumental music can be divided into two categories:

1. Listening music
2. Dance music

Listening music originally consisted of music that was composed to be played on an instrument or group of instruments solely for listening pleasure. Today, a good deal of the music that was originally performed for dancing is now played solely for listening, so this division has lost some of its meaning.

In this section of the chapter, we'll look at dance traditions as the major thread of instrumental music.

Irish whistle player Cathal McConnell.
PHOTO COURTESY: Flying Fish Records.

Dance Music

The most common dance music found in Great Britain and America is the *reel*, a word derived from the Anglo-Saxon *rulla* meaning to turn or whirl. The origins of the reel, a fast-paced dance performed to music in $\frac{4}{4}$ time, are unknown, but some believe it originated among the Celtic races that lived in England prior to the Anglo-Saxon raids and final domination of the English countryside. Both Ireland and Scotland claim to be the originators of the reel; certainly, both cultures have developed complicated tunes in this form.

The *hornpipe* is an ancient English form that was perhaps named for an ancient Celtic instrument, a single-reed wooden pipe fitted with a trumpet-like bell. The original hornpipe was danced to music in $\frac{3}{2}$ time (or triple rhythm), and probably was completely different than today's hornpipe, danced in $\frac{4}{4}$ (duple rhythm), and featuring elaborate footwork.

The *jig* is the final common form of British dance music, and also is a home-grown product. Jigs are usually in $\frac{6}{8}$ time, but also include tunes in $\frac{9}{8}$ and $\frac{12}{8}$.

The 18th and 19th centuries saw a great deal of musical activity in both Scotland and Ireland. At this time, a native Scottish dance form from the valley of the river Spey was introduced in Edinburgh. It was called the *strathspey* ["strath" means valley, "spey" is the name of the river]. Like the reel, it is written in $\frac{4}{4}$ time; however, it is performed at a more moderate tempo, and features many dotted rhythms.

Scot's Snaps

A sixteenth note followed by an eight note is the most common strathspey rhythm, and is called a Scott's snap; in playing this rhythm, the fiddler snaps the bow quickly, creating a jagged or broken sound.

In the 19th century, a wave of popular continental dances came to Great Britain, including the *waltz* (a slow dance in triple time), the *polka* (a moderately fast dance in double time), the *mazurka* (a round dance in triple time), and on and on. Most of these dances had Eastern European origins, and influenced classical music as well as folk dance.

Many of the British dance forms were brought to the United States by early immigrants to this country. The reel is the most popular form, found in both New England and throughout the South. Sometimes reel-type tunes are called "breakdowns" or "hoedowns." Jigs and hornpipes are more commonly found in New England and the Midwest than in the South. America has also contributed new tunes to the dance repertoire. Marching tunes composed during the Civil War entered into the folk tradition, at the beginning and close of a barndance, all of the participants might march around the hall, so that their fine clothing and good looks could be admired. American fiddlers developed a syncopated style of playing reels, perhaps influenced by Black American music, a style that emphasized rhythm and the sound of the fiddle bow over the melody. This contrasts with the British traditions that tend to be more melodic.

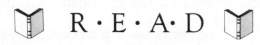

R·E·A·D

Bronson, Bertrand H., *The Ballad as Song*. Berkeley, CA: Univ. of California Press, 1969.

Bronson, Bertrand H., *The Singing Tradition of Child's Popular Ballads*. Princeton, NJ: Princeton University Press, 1976.

Chappell, William, *The Ballad Literature and Popular Music of the Olden Time*. New York: Dover Publications (reprint), 1965.

Child, Francis James, *The English and Scottish Popular Ballads*. New York: Dover Publications (reprint), 1965.

Gerrould, G. H., *The Ballad of Tradition*. London: Oxford University Press, 1932.

Kinsley, J., *The Oxford Book of Ballads* (2nd edition). London: Oxford University Press, 1969.

Sargent, H. C., and G. Kitman, *English and Scottish Popular Ballads*. Boston, MA: Houghton Mifflin and Co., 1932.

Simpson, Claude M., *The British Broadside Ballad and Its Music*. New Brunswick, NJ: Rutgers University Press, 1966.

Wells, Evelyn K., *The Ballad Tree*. London: Methuen, 1950.

L·I·S·T·E·N

Various, *The Unfortunate Rake: 16 Variants*. Folkways 3805.

Various, *Versions or Variants of "Barbara Allen."* Library of Congress, Archive of Folksong AFS L54.

3

British Isles traditions

In this chapter, we'll take a close look at the three great traditions of British Isles folk music: the music of England, Ireland, and Scotland. Actually, these divisions are fairly broad; within each general division, there are many different cultures and many different kinds of music. We'll begin by looking at the vocal traditions. Then, we'll look at the musical instruments that are common throughout the area, and finally at the instrumental music that is played on them.

Vocal Music

Vocal Style

In general, English singers tend to sing in a less ornamented style than their neighbors to the North (Scotland) or West (Wales, Ireland). They use less of the vocal "effects" (vibrato, slides, dips, glides) than these other singers. Also, they tend to use a less intense voice, or, in other words, they sing in a more relaxed style, closer to popular vocal style or the natural speaking voice.

Scottish singing is highly ornamented. Singers in both Gaelic and English traditions use many vocal ornaments, including glides, vibrato, and trills. The vocal chords are kept very tight, so that the sound of the voice is quite intense.

The Irish share with the Scots a love of ornamentation. However, they tend to sing with a less intense, less throaty sound. Instead, the Irish use a natural voice, with a lilting or sing-song style that is similar to the Irish speaking voice (called the Irish "brogue").

Song Types

The types of songs that are sung in England, Ireland, and Scotland have been outlined in Chapter II. However, in each area, singers have chosen specific types of songs that they prefer to sing over other types.

English Traditions. The English have developed a rich repertory of ritual songs, recently composed ballads (called "broadside ballads"), songs that relate to work and employment, and songs for and about recreation and amusement. Ritual songs are sung at a specific time of the year, to celebrate a particular festival such as May Day (to greet the spring) or at the winter solstice (at Christmas time).

The broadside ballads consist of ballads that were composed from the early 16th through the 19th century. These broadside ballads were printed on a single sheet of paper, usually accompanied by a simple, woodblock illustration, and served as a combination newspaper, story book, and popular magazine for the villagers and townsfolk. Because they sold for a penny, broadsides reached all levels of society.

Broadsides deal with news stories of the day, famous criminals, hangings, natural disasters, and romantic love. Broadside printers also published many traditional or classic ballads, helping them to survive to this century.

There is an entire group of songs that deal with work-related topics. These not only include the farming or rural songs, but also songs about mining, working in cotton mills, military life, navigation and sailing, and other songs that grew up with the growth of industry from the late 1700s on. Recreational songs include humorous songs sung to help pass the time after the work day was over. The English have a rich repertory of songs associated with the national pasttime, drinking.

One of the most famous English singers was recorded in the early years of this century by British folklorist/composer Percy Grainger. His name was Joseph Taylor (1833–?), and he came from Lincolnshire. Employed as a farm foreman, Taylor had a rich repertory of traditional ballads and songs. Unlike many other English singers, Taylor's singing was highly ornamented; one of his most stunning effects was a sudden switch from his normal singing voice to a high falsetto.

George Spicer (1906–   ), a sheep herder from Kent, is perhaps more typical of an English country singer. His repertory tends toward more modern ballads and comic songs, and even some songs from popular tradition. His singing voice is relaxed, with just the slightest hint of vibrato.

The Copper family are perhaps the most famous folksingers of

England. They have been shepherds for over 300 years in the same small village of Rottingdean near the English coast. A folklorist visited two of the singing Coppers in 1899, and ever since collectors have gone to the Copper farm to notate the hundreds of songs that are part of the family's tradition. The family repertory includes songs that tell of life on the farm, sheepherding, fox hunting, drinking, and courting: all integral parts of life for the average English workingman of the past five centuries. The Coppers are famous for another reason: when they sing together, they use harmony. It's not unusual for folksingers to sing together in unison, but it is quite unusual to hear two different parts (harmony). No one knows how this tradition began in the family.

Scottish Traditions. The Scottish culture is divided into two separate strands: the Gaelic culture that originally was the main force in Scottish life, and the newer English-language culture that was imported by the English to the South, and has taken over as the primary culture in most of Scotland.

The Gaelic singers preserve words and music that are several centuries old. Probably the oldest are the Gaelic ballads that tell the story of Ossian, the ancient Gaelic hero. These ballads are also occasionally found among English-speaking singers. Most of these songs are fragments of older epics, consisting of a few verses that have been remembered over the centuries (see Chapter 2).

Other Gaelic songs, including laments sung at funerals that recount the great deeds of a departed hero, and songs of praise that tell his story while he is still alive, were composed more recently, over the last few centuries. Scottish Gaelic culture was still strong up through the 1700s, and well-known composers worked for the Gaelic lords preserving not only their life stories but also, in the process, creating a body of music that has entered into the Gaelic tradition.

Most interesting of the Gaelic songs are the *waulking* songs, sung by women while they pound or stamp on newly woven cloth, in order to make the weave tighter. These songs are traditionally composed by women, and usually have short one- or two-line verses with a refrain made up either partially or entirely of nonsense words. A leader sings the verse and part of the refrain, and the group joins in on the body of the chorus. Like most work songs, waulking songs keep the group working together and help pass the time during this tedious task.

The English-speaking Scots are perhaps the greatest ballad singers of the British Isles. They have preserved many of the so-called "big" or classic ballads, called by the Scots the "muckle sangs" (literally, big songs). The classic ballads include the older narrative

Francis James Child, American ballad collector.

songs that have been collected by Francis James Child and other folklorists. At the turn of this century, Scottish folklorist Gavin Grieg recorded over 3,000 traditional songs in Northeastern Scotland, almost all of which were ballads.

There are many Scottish singers who have been recorded over the past half-century. One of the most famous is Jeannie Robertson, from the town of Aberdeen. Robertson's singing showed great precision, almost as if she had trained herself in singing the "big ballads" just like an opera singer prepares to sing the great arias. Another great singer from the same area was John Strachan, from the town of Fyvie, whose singing was powerful, with a healthy dose of humor.

Another class of song found among the Lowland Scots is associated with the life of the roving farmers. Farm hands were hired at county fairs by owners of large estates, and would work for a single season performing the heavy labor necessary to bring in the crops. Male farmers lived in large dormitories called *bothies*. Out of the bothy came a group of songs describing farm life known as bothy ballads. These are not true ballads, but include songs for amusement, drinking songs, love songs, and songs that comment on the hired man's plight. One of the great bothy singers was Jimmy McBeath, whose repertory of songs focused entirely on life on the farm.

Irish traditions. Irish culture is also split between Gaelic and English speakers. However, in Ireland, most English speakers also know some Gaelic, and it is common to find singers who sing in both languages. The Irish Gaelic songs are most commonly lyrical laments, describing the plight of true love gone wrong, or the passing of a great hero or period of Irish history. The emphasis is on the mood of sadness itself, rather than the story the song might tell.

The English-language Irish songs include the same classic and more recently composed ballads known in England and Scotland. The history of Ireland is one made up of continual struggle with the English, who have sought to colonize and dominate the original Irish culture. For this reason, songs that tell the story of Irish history, oppression, and the various uprisings and rebellions are quite popular. These national songs can be heard everywhere from the backroom of a pub to the assembly rooms of the Irish government to the concert stage in Ireland and abroad.

Joe Heaney (1920–   ) is representative of many Irish singers, in that he sings songs in both Gaelic and English. Irish singers have to be able to move comfortably between the two traditions. Heaney carries the Gaelic style of ornamentation and delivery to his singing of English-language songs. Others do the opposite, singing the Gaelic songs in a flat, unornamented style influenced by their training in the English singing traditions.

Musical Instruments

Musicologists have often wondered what are the oldest musical instruments found in the British Isles. If we go back just 300 years, we might find totally different instruments than are played today, even though many of these would share the same names with today's folk instruments. In this section, we'll focus on the instruments as they are played today, although we will note the history of each instrument and how it has changed over the years.

There can be no doubt that the oldest types of musical instruments found in this area are the plucked harp, the bagpipe, and the bowed lute (or fiddle). Even these instruments date back only about 1,000 years. We can only speculate as to the nature of earlier instruments, which would probably include simple whistles and drums.

The Harp

When we think of the harp today, we think of the full-scale concert harp used in classical music. This modern harp was developed from many earlier sources in the 19th century. The folk harps that we will be describing here date back to about the 12th to 14th centuries, and survived in tradition until the late 18th century.

By definition, a harp has strings running at a right angle to the body of the instrument. The earliest harps found in the British Isles (predating the 12th century) probably consisted of nothing more than a simple soundbox with a neck attached to either end.

Somewhere in the time between the 12th to 14th centuries, a pillar was added to the basic harp design. This harp was called the *clarsach*, and probably originated in Ireland. The most famous example is the "Brian Boru" harp, named for a legendary Irish musician, dating from the 14th century. It had wire strings, which were plucked with the backs of long fingernails.

The Scottish clarsach is similar to the Irish, with a slightly higher point or hump at the meeting of the neck and pillar. Scottish harps were strung with either wire or gut strings. The Welsh developed their own type of harp, probably sometime in the 16th century. This featured a tall, straight pillar, and a gently curving neck. It was known as the "triple harp" because it featured three rows of strings: two rows tuned in unison or in octaves, and one additional row to play semitones.

From the 11th to the 16th centuries, harpers played an important role in the lord's hall. However, by the late 17th century, the power of the lords had diminished. The harpers had to take to the road, and earned a meager living by performing wherever a friendly crowd could be assembled, in country inns, at fairs, and occasionally at the home of a wealthy person. Usually the harpers were blind; unable to find any other work due to their handicap, they were the last in a line of what was once a noble profession.

Over the centuries, Ireland and Scotland developed their own elaborate harp styles. The most famous Irish harpist/composer was Turlough O'Carolan (c. 1670–1738). Born blind, O'Carolan travelled from lord to lord, composing both music and poetry in praise of his benefactors. Today, his compositions such as "Sheebeg Sheemore" and "Carolan's Concerto" are favorites among folk musicians.

The Bagpipes

The bagpipes are second only to the harp as the greatest folk instrument of the British Isles. English, Irish, and Scottish musicians originally played mouthblown bagpipes; that is, the player blew into a small tube, connected to a sack (often made out of an animal's skin), that filled with air. The air was then forced from the sack into another pipe (or a number of pipes) that contained reeds. *Drone* pipes play only one note; they have no finger holes, so their tone cannot be changed. The *chanter*, or melody pipe, has finger holes, and by changing the fingering, the player can play different notes. This form of bagpipe probably dates back 1,000 years.

Sometime over the last centuries, a second form of bagpipe developed. Instead of blowing into a pipe, the player squeezed a set of bellows, much like the bellows you might use to stoke a fire. The bellows provided the air needed to inflate the bag.

Oddly enough, although all three cultures knew both types of bagpipes, sometime in the 18th century each area adopted its own type of instrument. The English seem to have abandoned the bagpipes, although in one northern region, Northumbria, a small bellows-blown bagpipe is played to this day. One of the greatest masters of the Northumbrian smallpipes was Billy Pigg. His playing typically featured many elaborate arpeggios and scale runs, executed with dazzling speed and precision.

Sam Bennett, Morris dance fiddler from Ilmington, Warwickshire, England. c. 1900. Reproduction from the Collections of the Library of Congress.

The bellows-blown pipes became the national instrument of Ireland. The Irish developed an elaborate type of bagpipes now called the *uillean* or union pipes, featuring bellows to provide the air power, a chanter, drones, and another set of pipes called *regulators*, that played chords instead of just single notes. Some players don't use the regulators at all. The Irish pipes are so complicated that they take years to master, and great players are few and far between.

The Scottish developed the mouth-blown Highland pipes, which are so loud that they can be heard for miles. The Scottish pipes played two major roles: as a battle cry before an important battle, and as the voice of lamentation at the funeral of a famous warrior or lord. The Scottish developed bagpipe music to its greatest level in the traditional *piobaireacd* (often called *pibroch*), the music that the Scottish themselves called *ceol mor* (or "the great music"). Pibroch serves as music for gatherings, military battles, and, most commonly, as a form of lament. The pibroch opens with a slow-moving statement of the melody, called in Gaelic the *urlar* or ground. This is followed by three sections of variations, in which the speed and complexity of the melody picks up.

The great Scottish pipers learned their music through a system of vocables (or sung notes) called *canntaireachd*. By singing these syllables, the pipers learn complex melodies without ever reading a note of music. This form of "notation" helped keep pibroch alive. Today, unlike the classical harp traditions of Ireland, pibroch continues to be performed by pipers who have learned the music through the oral tradition in an unbroken chain back through the centuries.

The Fiddle

The fiddle has a long and interesting history. Today, fiddlers play an instrument that is identical to the classical violin. Previously, medieval bowed instruments had come to the area from Europe, including the medieval fiddle (sometimes spelled *fedyl* or *fidil*) and the *rebec*. Both were earlier forms of bowed instruments, and neither were native to the British Isles. In the 16th century, the *viol*, an earlier form of violin popular in Europe, came to the region and was quickly adopted at court. Finally, the violin as we know it today was introduced sometime in the 18th century.

There is one bowed instrument that is believed to be native to the British Isles. It is known as the Welsh *crwth* (called *crowd* in England and *crot* or *cruit* in Ireland). At one time it was known throughout the British Isles; however, it has not survived to today, although Welsh crwth players performed as late as the middle of the 19th century. In this Welsh form, it was both plucked and bowed, and featured a nearly rectangular body divided into two parts. The lower half consisted of a sound box, the upper half of an open frame. Eventually, this instrument was supplanted by the modern violin, with its brighter sound and better playing features.

The violin traditions heard in the British Isles show a wide variety of styles. The English tend to play in an unornamented style, and few "virtuoso" players have been recorded. In Ireland, a tradition of fiddle playing has grown up that is highly ornate, demanding a great deal of bowing and fingering skill. Perhaps the best-known Irish fiddler is Sligo-born Michael Coleman (1891–1945), who emigrated to the United States in the early years of the 20th century, and recorded many 78 records that spread his style throughout the world. The Scots also have a virtuostic fiddle tradition. Fiddler J. Scott Skinner (1843–1927) is one of the best-known Scottish fiddle masters and composers, whose motto "Talent does what it may; genius does what it must" sums up his own high standards of performance.

Other Instruments

There are many other instruments that have been part of the British Isles folk tradition. End-blown flutes (including fifes and pennywhistles) are common, while the transverse (or side-blown) wooden flute, introduced in the classical world in the early 18th century, remains popular, particularly in Ireland. This flute features

From l. to r., Irish or *uillean* bagpipes, wooden (open-hole) flute, and *bodhran* (Irish frame drum).
PHOTO COURTESY: Green Linnet Records.

six open holes; some models also feature keys to extend the range of the instrument. The modern Boehm-system flute has not been as widely adopted in folk circles.

Other stringed instruments (besides the violin) include the tenor banjo, mandolin, and guitar, all introduced over the last 150 years. The hammer dulcimer, a member of the zither family, is one of the older folk instruments, dating back some 500 years or so, and is still played by individual musicians in England, Scotland, and Ireland.

Reed instruments and trumpets are less common in the folk world. One type of reed instrument, called free-reeds, is quite popular, thanks to a number of 19th-century inventions, including the accordion, melodian, and concertina.

Drums are rarer, although the Irish play a frame drum called the bodhran, which resembles a large tambourine. Bodhrans are played with a special double-ended stick. By flicking this stick rapidly back and forth, the player is able to create complex rhythms.

Instrumental/Dance Music

There are two major types of dance performed in the British Isles: (1) imitative dances; and (2) recreational dances. Imitative dances involve the imitation of animal movements, ritual sacrifice, or other ancient customs associated with religious rituals that were once part of a native British religion. Recreational dances developed more recently, and include all dances that are performed solely for fun.

The English have the most unusual imitative dance tradition, the Morris dance. All three cultures share a type of recreational dance known as the country dance. The Scots and Irish have also developed unique solo and group dance forms, involving elaborate footwork; I have grouped these dances together under the heading of step dances.

Morris Dance

Morris dancing is a traditional dance of England that is many centuries old. No one knows where the name "Morris dance" comes from; there are some people who believe the dance comes from the Moors of North Africa, and "Morris" is a corruption of the word "Moorish." However, dances similar to the Morris tradition are found throughout Europe, so that the history of this particular dance form will probably always remain mysterious.

Six men, three to a row, perform the dance. In some dances,

they hold tree limbs or sticks, clashing the sticks together during the chorus part of the dance. In other dances, they twirl handkerchiefs over their heads as they dance. Non-dancers are also involved with the Morris dance; they include a "Maid Marian" (a man dressed as a woman) and a "fool," who moves among the dancers, carrying a bladder on a stick that he beats against the ground.

The Morris dance is traditionally accompanied by pipe (a short, three-holed whistle) and tabor (a small framedrum), fiddle, or, beginning in the 19th century, concertina. Many of today's Morris dance melodies are based on country dance tunes first heard in the 1600s; some folklorists believe that the original Morris tunes have been lost. Traditionally, it was only performed at Whitsuntide (in mid-May), as part of the early spring rituals celebrating the rebirth of the Earth after winter.

Morris dancers may also perform sword dances (performed either with stiff metal rods or flexible rapiers). The sword dance is in turn associated with an ancient mummer's play, telling of the life and death of the mythical hero, St. George, the patron saint of England who died slaying a monstrous dragon, and was magically reborn. Many people believe that the play and dances are all part of an ancient religious ritual that is now remembered only through these fragments.

Morris dancing would probably be unknown today if not for the work of two men: folklorist Cecil Sharp (1859–1924) and dancer/musician William Kimber (1872–1961). Kimber came from Headington Quarry, a small town near Oxford, where most of the men were employed either mining the famous "Headington hard" stone used in buildings throughout the area or as masons. Early on, Kimber learned the building trades from his father, along with his vast repertory of Morris tunes and dances. The Headington Quarry Morris dance team was very active throughout the last years of the 19th century, but by 1899 the team had fallen on hard times. Many of the men were out of work, and there was no longer much interest in traditional dance among the villagers. In order to raise some spare change, the team decided to perform at Christmas time of that year. Coincidentally, when Cecil Sharp was visiting relatives in the area, he saw the dancing, realized that it was something quite beautiful and unusual, and invited Kimber to dance for him.

Sharp notated many of the Morris dances from throughout England, wrote several books on Morris dance style, and lectured, accompanied by Kimber who would demonstrate the dances and play the tunes. Soon, local Morris teams were being revived, and a new team formed.

Bidford Morris Dancers at Redditch, June 1906 with John Robbins, musician.
PHOTO COURTESY: English Folk Dance and Song Society

Country Dance

The dance music of Great Britain that we know today has developed over the last five centuries. During this period, there were several important outside influences. The court of Louis XIV of France had a great impact on European dance music; it was in this period that dancing masters took traditional dances from the countryside and made them more appealing to the nobility by smoothing out the rhythms, making the movements more graceful, and arranging the music for court instruments.

England has its own national dance, the country dance, a broad range of dances that are performed in the English countryside, including dances performed in lines, circles, or square formations. *Contra dance* is a term that has grown up in New England to describe traditional English dances performed in two parallel lines. A large part of the English country dance repertory consists of contras.

Melodies and instructions for country dances were noted by an English publisher named John Playford (1623–c. 1687). His collection, first published in 1651, gained such great popularity that today these dances are called "Playford dances." The country dance was exported to France (where it was called *contre danse*) and the continent, and the refinements of the French dancing masters were in turn passed back to England.

Step Dance

The Scots and Irish have developed elaborate step dances, performed either as solo dances or as part of the country dance tradition. These developments occurred over the last 300 years or so.

The Scottish tradition is more of a social than a solo one. They have taken the country dance and added new twists to the figures and new movements to the feet. Instead of merely walking around the floor, as you do in square dancing, the Scots have added elaborate skipping steps and other specialized steps. Special dances have become associated with particular tunes.

Irish step dancing was spread by dancing masters who travelled from town to town teaching the elaborate techniques involved in mastering the steps. Step dancing is the grandfather of American tap dancing, and is similar to tap in that it involves elaborate foot and leg movements, performed while keeping the rest of the body stiff.

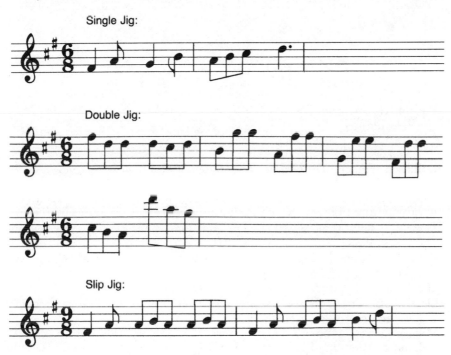

Many step dances are performed to the music of the jig, a dance rhythm in either $\frac{6}{8}$, $\frac{9}{8}$, or $\frac{12}{8}$ time. The Irish developed an elaborate system of jigs in the 18th century, distinguishing among single, double, and slip jigs, according to the dance steps that were performed to the music.

In Irish step dancing, the dancer slaps the floor with the toe and heel of his foot. In a single jig, the dancer makes only a single slapping (or what the Irish call "battering") movement; the music features a quarter note followed by an eighth (on which the slap occurs). In a double jig, the music features three eighth notes in a row; the dancer batters the floor twice, once on the second eighth note, and once on the third eighth note. This double battering gives the jig its name. Slip or hop jigs, usually in $\frac{9}{8}$ time, feature a different type of step, involving a sliding of the foot across the floor. Slides, performed to tunes in $\frac{12}{8}$ time and commonly only found in Kerry, involve yet a different type of sliding step.

Jigs are primarily performed by virtuoso solo dancers, and are designed to show off the individual's fancy footwork. Another dance form, called the set dance, developed to allow individual steppers to dance together, performing complicated figures along with the intricate foot movement. Set dance tunes were composed in a variety of different rhythms to accompany these dances.

R · E · A · D

Breathnach, Brendan, *Folk Music and Dances of Ireland*. Dublin: Mercier Press, 1971, 1980.

Collinson, Francis, *The Traditional and National Music of Scotland*. Boston, MA: Routledge and Kegan Paul, 1966.

Collinson, Francis, *The Bagpipe: The History of a Musical Instrument*. London: Routledge and Kegan Paul, 1975.

Grattan Flood, William H., *The Story of the Bagpipe*. London: Walter Scott Publishing Co., 1911.

Karpeles, Maud, *Cecil Sharp, His Life and Work*. Chicago, IL: University of Chicago Press, 1967.

Kidson, Frank and Mary Neal, *English Folk Song and Dance*. Cambridge: Cambridge University Press, 1915.

Lloyd, A. L., *Folksong in England*. New York: International Publishers, 1967.

Lloyd, A. L., *Come All Ye Bold Miners: Ballads and Songs of the Coalfields*. London: Lawrence and Wishart, 1978.

Milligan, Jean C., *Won't You Join the Dance: The Scottish Country Dance Manual*. London: Paterson's Publications, 1982.

Ord, James, *Bothy Ballads*. Hatboro, PA. Folklore Associates, 1965.
Sharp, Cecil, *English Folk Song: Some Conclusions*. (3rd ed.). London: Methuen, 1954.
Williams, Alfred, *Folk Songs of the Upper Thames*. London: Duckworth, 1923.
Williams, Iola, *English Folk Dance and Song*. London: Longmans Green & Co., 1935.

 L·I·S·T·E·N

Vocal Music

A. ENGLAND
Cox, Harry. Folk Legacy 20
Jordan, Fred, *Songs of a Shropshire Farmer*. Topic 150
Larner, Sam, *A Garland for Sam*. Topic 244
Spicer, George, *Blackberry Fold*. Topic 235
Various, *English Folk Songs*. CBS Special Products 4943
Various, *Folksongs of Britain, Vols. 1–10*. Topic 157–161, 194–198
Various, *The Borders*. Folkways

B. IRELAND
Heaney, Joe, *Irish Traditional Songs*. Topic 91
Heaney, Joe and Gabe O'Sullivan, *Joe and the Gabe*. Green Linnet 1018
Tunney, Paddy. Folk Legacy 7
Tunney, Paddy, *A Wild Bee's Nest*. Topic 139
Various, *Field Trip*. Folkways 8872
Various, *Irish Folk Songs*. CBS Special Products 4941
Various, *The Lark in the Morning*. Tradition 1004
Various, *Traditional Music of Ireland, Vols. 1 & 2*. Folkways 8781/8782

C. SCOTLAND
Higgins, Lizzie, *Princess of the Thistle*. Topic 185
Kennedy, Norman. Folk Legacy 34
McBeath, Jimmy, *Wild Rover No More*. Topic 173
Robertson, Jeannie. Topic 96
Stewart Family, *The Traveling Stewarts*. Topic 179
Various, *Bothy Ballads*. Tangent 109
Various, *Folk Songs from Scotland*. CBS Special Products 4946
Various, *Gaelic Psalms from Lewis*. Tangent 120
Various, *Heather & Glen*. Tradition 1047
Various, *Music from the Western Isles*. Tangent 110
Various, *Songs and Pipes of the Hebrides*. Folkways 4430
Various, *The Muckle Sangs (Big Ballads)*. Tangent 119/D
Various, *Waulking Songs from Barra*. Tangent 111

Instrumental Traditions

A. ENGLAND
Anderson, Alistair, *Dookin for Apples*. Front Hall 020
Kimber, William, *The Art of William Kimber*. Topic 249
Old Swan Band, *Gamesters, Pickpockets & Harlots*. Dingles 322
Pyewackett. Dingles 312
Swarbrick, Dave. Kicking Mule 337
Various, *Boscastle Breakdown*. Topic 240
Various, *Wild Hills of Wannie*. Topic 227

B. IRELAND
Bell, Derek, *Carolan's Favorite*. Shanachie 79020
Coleman, Michael, *Classic Recordings*. Shanachie 33006
Coleman, Michael, *The Legacy*. Shanachie 33002
Ennis, Seamus, *40 Years of Irish Piping*. Green Linnet 1000
Killoran, Paddy, *Back in Town*. Shanachie 33003
McConnell, Cathal, *On Lough Erne's Shore*. Flying Fish 27058
McGuire, Seamus and Manus, *Humours of Lissadell*. Folk Legacy 78
Murphy, Dennis and Julia Clifford. Claddagh CC5
Peoples, Tommy, *The High Part of the Road*. Shanachie 29003
Rea, John, *Irish Music on the Hammer Dulcimer*. Topic 373
Rowsome, Leo, *Classics of Irish Piping, Vols. 1 & 2*. Topic 259, 322
Various, *Irish Dance Music*. Folkways 8821
Various, *Irish Jigs, Reels & Hornpipes*. Folkways 6819
Various, *Irish Popular Dances*. Folkways 6818
Various, *Lady of the House*. Shanachie 33005
Various, *Sailing Into Walpole's Marsh*. Green Linnet 1004
Various, *The Lark in The Clear Air*. Topic 230
Various, *The Wheels of the World*. Shanachie 33001

C. SCOTLAND
Battlefield Band, *Home is Where the Van Is*. Flying Fish 250
Cameron Men. Topic 321
Kinnard, Alison, *The Harp Key*. Temple 001
Lamey, Bill, *Scottish Fiddle*. Shanachie 14002
Skinner, J. Scott, *The Strathspey King*. Topic 280
Various, *Scottish Fiddlers to the Fore*. BBC REB 84M
Various, *Shetland Fiddle Music*. Tangent 117

4

Folk music in a new land

The United States is a country of many different cultures that have come together to form a new culture. We have seen that the folk music of the British Isles is quite complex; even within a single area, such as Ireland, there are many different regional styles that exist, with wide varieties in singing and instrumental styles. You would expect that in the United States, where so many cultures have come together to form a new country, that the folk music would be even more complex—and you'd be right!

Who Are These Folk?

We have to pose this question again: Who are the "folk" in the folk music of the United States?

The original "folk" were the Indians. They came to this continent first, and we assume were the first Americans. If you are interested in the music of the Indians, you should look back at Volume I of this series, *Man's Earliest Music*, which gives an overview of American Indian music. Indian music is usually studied separately from American folk music, because it is so different from either the British or the African traditions that make up the mainstream of American music.

The first wave of emigrants to the U.S. included the British, Spanish, and French who came to colonize the continent during the 16th, 17th, and 18th centuries. Because the British were most

45

successful in settling this continent, their culture, including their folk music, became the dominant force in America. There still are areas where you can hear French and Spanish folk musics, the French in Canada and Northern New England, and in a small pocket in Louisiana, and the Spanish in the Southwest. However, even in these areas the British influence is great.

Besides the British influence, the second important factor in American folk music came from Africa. The slave trade was established in the earliest years of the conquest of the American continent. Africans were brought to this country as slaves to work on the large farms of the South and to help out in the homes of the North. The Africans brought with them musical instruments, singing styles, song subjects, and a different approach to rhythm than was ever heard in Europe. Without this strong African influence, American folk music would be quite different today.

Melting Pot or Stew Pot?

Besides the mainstream American folk music, there are many other folk musics that are heard in America. As new emigrants came to this country through the 19th and early 20th century, they brought with them their cultures. Immigrants settled in country and town, worked in factories and on farms, moved from the East coast (where many of them first entered this country) out to every corner of the continent.

America has often been described as a "melting pot" of cultures. Imagine a large cauldron over a fire. As each new culture came to this country, it was mixed into the contents of the pot. The individual characteristics of these peoples were "melted down" into a new character, the American way of living. Italian, German, French, Scandinavian, Chinese, Syrian, Russian, the people of these cultures came to America, abandoned their languages, their traditional ways of dressing, their old jobs, even, in some cases, their families and marriages, to make a new life in America. And it is true that in America there is a national culture that ties people from all over the world together.

However, there is another way of looking at American life. I like to think of this as the "stew pot" rather than the "melting pot." Again, imagine people coming from all corners of the earth. As they come to America, they all join the same stew. Each culture brings its own unique way of life, including language, song, dress, art, occupation, and talents. These individual aspects and qualities add new flavors to the stew. And although everyone joins in the stew, each person also keeps an individual identity in it. When you eat a stew, it has one overall flavor and texture, but you can still recognize a carrot, and know that it is different from a potato or an onion. Similarly, in the United States today, you can still find Hungarians who speak their native language, dress in native clothing, and perform Hungarian music, even through these same people actively participate in American life. The same is true for many other peoples.

Whatever image you use to describe American culture—whether it is a stew; a quilt, made up of many different "patches" (or cultures) sewn together to form a blanket; or a rainbow, an arc made up of many different colors, each one unique, but all joined together into a single strand—it is important to remember that America is a country of many different peoples, and that its folk music reflects the influence of different cultures coming together to form something new, an American way of singing, playing musical instruments, and creating new songs.

Making the Stew

Immigrants to America have found a country of wide-open spaces, where they could settle peacefully and continue to practice age-old customs without interference from their neighbors or the government. On the other hand, they have found tightly packed cities, where different cultures could come together and communicate in ways that they never did before. In the 19th century, newspapers, travelling teachers, and road shows brought new trends to even the most isolated parts of the country. In the 20th century, radio, records, and television have played a major role in spreading different cultures from one end of the continent to the other—and throughout the world.

Some examples may help you understand the rich interchange among cultures that has occurred in America. Bruno Nettl has described how one of the most isolated groups in this country, the Amish, have been influenced by other cultures. When we think of the Amish, we think of a group of people who are determined to continue to live in an old-fashioned way. They have settled in Pennsylvania, where they maintain farms using horses and mules to draw their plows. They don't believe in the "modern conveniences," and don't actively participate in modern American life.

Nettl describes two types of Amish music, both associated with their religion: one is an ancient style of hymn singing, and the other is made up of recently composed songs. These two different types of Amish music underscore two important influences on their culture: isolation and participation.

The ancient hymns sung by the Amish are like no other songs in the world. The hymns are sung very slowly, so slowly that they barely seem to have any rhythm or beat. The words of the hymns are broken down into syllables; instead of one syllable being accompanied by one note of the melody, each syllable is stretched out to be sung over many notes. Words, notes, and rhythms move ahead very slowly. Nettl describes this music as unlike any other that you might imagine hearing in the United States or Europe.

Oddly enough, this ancient Amish style of singing hymns was not imported by the Amish from Europe, as far as we can tell. No one sings in this style in the Amish homelands of Germany today. It is possible that the Amish have preserved an ancient style of singing that was at one time popular in Germany. The other possibility is that, in their isolation, they have developed thier own way of singing that is unique to them.

Isolation—or living apart from other people—is an important influence on many different cultures in the United States. Because this is such a big country, and, until recently, not a very crowded one, there was always room for different peoples to strike out on their own. When a culture is isolated, it tends to either preserve earlier forms of singing, dance, or instrumental music, or to create individual variations of traditional musical forms.

Although a culture may appear to be isolated, there are many ways in which American culture has reached into even the most determinedly isolated communities. Again, we can turn to the Amish and look at their second singing tradition, the more modern hymns. These hymns shows the influence of the German culture from which the Amish emigrated to this country, as you might expect. But they also show the influece of the early 19th century British and American hymns that the Amish heard when they came to this country. The Amish have even adopted American popular songs, taking the melody of "The Battle Hymn of the Republic" and crafting new words to it. Printed hymn books and professional hymn writers had their impact on the Amish, and new songs were added to their repertory from the wealth of composed music.

Participation, or joining in the American community, has changed Amish culture and music, just as much as isolation has helped preserve their culture. It may seem amazing to you that a culture can be both isolated and at the same time a part of the American mainstream. Here's an example from my personal experience.

When I was a college student, I attended school in Oberlin,

Ohio. I was interested in folk music and heard that there were some talented Irish musicians living in Cleveland, a large industrial city. Through the local Irish-American club, I contacted some of these musicians, and arranged to attend a "session," or a night of friendly music playing, in the basement of one of their homes. This was the beginning of my exposure to a rich Irish culture that had survived in the Midwest.

Stepping into the home of this Irish musician was like stepping out of America back into Ireland. On the table was a spread of Irish homemade breads and pastries. In the basement, a group of older men were assembled, some fiddle players, some flute players, all speaking with rich Irish accents. They played the traditional dance music of Ireland, pausing occasionally to share a drink, a story, or a joke. At first, they distrusted me and my friends; we had longer hair and beards, were dressed like young hippies, and didn't look at all like the type of people who they thought would be interested in their music. But, as soon as we started to play along with them, we were welcomed warmly into the special inner circle of musicians.

I became friendly with two of the musicians that I met that night. One was a flute player who worked as a foreman at the large railroad yards in downtown Cleveland. His job was to supervise the loading and unloading of freight cars as they passed through this important rail connection to the East and West. He had 11 children, none of whom spoke Gaelic (the traditional language of Ireland), and none of whom played Irish music. When I visited his home to enjoy a session of music, his children were either

Tom Byrne (flute) &
Tom McCaffrey (fiddle).
PHOTOGRAPH: Richard Carlin.

watching TV or listening to Fleetwood Mac records on the stereo. Only the eight-year-old son expressed any interest in the music that his father played.

The second musician was a fiddle player, story teller, and singer of sentimental and comic songs. He was a bachelor who worked as a ground's supervisor at a local high school, picking up trash, mowing the lawn, and caring for the trees and plants. His father had been a fiddler before him, and his grandfather before his father, and he had learned at his father's knee the tunes that had always been played in his family. He also learned tunes from records and the radio, so that his repertory was a mix of the old and the new. But, everything that he played had the stamp of his own personal style on it, always with a touch of humor and good-natured fun, an important aspect of his personality.

The Irish neighborhood in Cleveland is in some ways very isolated. Young boys skateboard down the hilly streets, unafraid of traffic. People sit out on the porches of their small frame houses during the summer months, gossiping with each other just like they lived in a tiny village in Ireland. There isn't any feeling of the urban decay, crime, and general poor living conditions that are found in some other parts of the city.

On the other hand, neither musician who I knew was isolated from American life. Both were proud U.S. citizens. Although they were proud to be Irish, they were equally proud to participate in American life, hotly debating local and national politics. Both were concerned that the young Irish people continue to practice Irish music and culture, but were also concerned that they be successful in America, owning bigger houses, having better jobs, and getting a better education than their fathers.

Musically, both men were interested in the latest musical trends, although neither played popular music. They learned tunes by ear from other musicians, just as had been done in Ireland for centuries, but also took advantage of modern conveniences such as phonographs and cassette players to help them learn from musicians they had never met. In Ireland, it would be unusual for a villager from Donegal to hear a musician from another town, simply because travel was limited. Hard labor on the farm left little time or energy for travel from town to town. In America, thanks to phonograph records and the mixing of peoples from different parts of Ireland in single neighborhoods, Irish musicians were able to swap ideas from all over the countryside.

In many ways, these Irish immigrants were isolated from the rest of the country. They maintained Irish culture in the face of great pressures to conform, to be "American" rather than to continue to be Irish. However, in another sense they were very much a part of American life. At the work place, my Irish flute-player friend supervised Hungarians, Germans, Scots, Welsh, Indians (from India, not Native Americans), and other Irishmen. In a single night in Cleveland you could hear Greek music, music from the South of India, Hungarian orchestras, rock 'n' roll bands playing Top 40 music, the Cleveland Symphony playing the classical music of Europe, and my Irish friends playing the dance music of their homeland.

Charting the Immigrant Traditions

You would have to draw a pretty complicated map to show all of the various immigrants who have come to the United States, and where they settled. However, I would like to sketch in broadly some of the important groups.

In the Northeast and Southeast, where the original 13 colonies were located, you'll find the strongest surviving British traditions: ballad singing, lyric songs, and dance music. Although the British tradition had a lasting impact on the entire country, this is the area where most traditional British music has survived. In the Southeast, there is another, and very important, tradition: Black-American music. Black slaves were brought to all parts of the country, but they had the greatest impact musically in the Southern states.

Along the Southern border of the country, particularly in Texas, we find another important influence: Mexican or Spanish music. This musical blend is popularly known as Tex-Mex music. In the industrial cities of the North, from upstate New York across the country to Minneapolis, we find many of the European immigrant cultures: Irish, German, Hungarian, and Polish. In the Eastern cities, such as New York, we find other immigrant cultures, such as Jewish and Italian groups.

Of course, there are also scattered around the country many smaller groups who have had a large impact musically. However, these are some of the main groups that we'll be focussing on.

In the following chapters, we'll look at some of these traditions in more detail. First, we'll examine the two strongest influences: the British and African traditions. We'll then examine some of the many rich immigrant musics that continue to be performed in the U.S. Finally, we'll take a brief look at commercial country music, the folk music "revival," and how folk music continues to play an important role in American life.

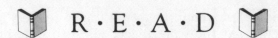 R · E · A · D

Nettl, Bruno, *An Introduction to Folk Music in the United States*. Detroit, MI: Wayne State University Press, 1972.

Nettl, Bruno, *Folk and Traditional Music of the Western Continents* (2nd edition). Englewood Cliffs, NJ: Prentice-Hall, 1973.

 L · I · S · T · E · N

Byrne, Tom and Tom McCaffery, *Irish Music in Cleveland, Vols. 1–3*. Folkways 3517, 3521, 3523

5

Britain in the U.S.

Style and Songs

The original British settlers brought with them two important elements that would become a part of American folk traditions: style (or the way that music is performed) and song (or the actual repertory or group of songs that are performed). Bill Malone, in an excellent book called *Country Music U.S.A.*, points out that even if people forget the individual songs that were sung at one time, the style of singing will live on. Let's take a look at this style.

Style

As we discussed in Chapter 3, English, Irish, and Scottish singers all have different singing styles. Some sing in a highly ornamented manner, some with little or no ornamentation; some keep their throats tight, producing a nasal, sharper pitch, while others sing in a relaxed style, keeping their throats open, producing a smoother sound. These same variations in singing style are found from New England down through the Southern mountains. Sometimes an individual singer will sing in a totally different manner than any of his or her neighbors. A regional style can be limited to a handful of singers or embrace a large number of musicians found in the same general area.

One of the first folklorists to collect traditional music in America was a foreigner, Cecil Sharp, the famous British folklorist who was so important in the preserving of traditional English Morris dance. He came to the Southern mountains in 1916 to see if British traditional songs and ballads had survived in the New World. The result was one of the first great collections of American folksong.

Sharp made an interesting observation when he recorded Southern singers. He found that they sang many modern songs, as well as the traditional ballads that dated back many centuries. However, when they sang these modern songs, something unusual happened. The modern song was changed, so that it sounded like a folksong. In Sharp's words, "When . . . a modern street-song succeeds in penetrating into the mountains it is at once mated to a traditional tune and sometimes still further purified by being moulded into the form of a traditional ballad."

One example of how a traditional singer takes a modern song and molds it into a traditional style can be heard on "The End of an Old Song," a record of ballad singer Dillard Chandler made by John Cohen (1932–   ), an American folklorist. Chandler is a farmer from North Carolina who ekes out a living in the mountains. He sings with a powerful voice that is piercing, sharp, and throaty. Chandler learned many of his songs from his relatives and other traditional singers; but, he has also learned songs from the radio, including an Elvis Presley song about the death of a faithful dog, called "Old Shep." Although this is a modern song, Chandler makes it sound like an ancient ballad by the way that he sings it.

Songs

The repertory or group of songs and dance tunes that has come from Britain is a very rich one. It includes the traditional ballads that tell stories of family strife, love gone wrong, magicians, monsters, and maidens in distress. In many cases, the names of towns and heroes and heroines have been changed, to give a local, American interest to the stories. Some of the ballads have shrunk, with entire sections of the songs being eliminated as singers either forget, or choose to shorten, the ancient songs. The broadside ballads of the 18th century, composed songs that relate the events of the day, are also found in America. And the many lyric songs, expressing all human emotions, have survived in the New World.

There are several types of ballads that are new to the U.S. traditions. First, there are ballads that tell the story of local events, particularly of natural disasters. These are similar to the British broadside ballads (see Chapter 3) in that they are recently composed, and are often written to be sung to older traditional tunes. A flood, fire, or other spectacular natural disaster will often be the subject of a ballad. A second type of ballad that is unique to America is the "blues ballad"; this combines the story-telling style of a ballad with the sad, lonesome feeling of a blues. One of the most famous blues ballads is "Frankie and Johnnie," telling the story of a betrayed female (Frankie) who takes her revenge on her ex-lover (Johnnie) by shooting him.

In the South, sentimental ballads and songs became popular around the turn of the century. At this time, the building of new factories led many young farmers to abandon the land and to take jobs in the mills and mines. Living in company towns or big cities, the new generation of workers and their families felt cut off from the older mountain traditions. The sentimental songs express a longing for a simpler life, the kind of life that was lived before the coming of the machine age. They often deal with home, the family, the sweetheart left behind, or dear mother, old and gray.

Another important influence on traditional singers was the travelling minstrel and tent shows. These shows brought professional entertainment to the tiniest hamlets, and also carried the latest, professionally composed songs. The music of Stephen Foster (1826–1864) was introduced by travelling minstrels, and swept the country in the second half of the 19th century. Today we consider his songs, including "Swanee River," "Camptown Races," and "Oh Susanna," to be folk songs, even though we know who composed them. These songs served as models for new folk compositions, introducing more modern ideas about melody, rhythm, and harmony.

Regional Differences

There are regional differences in the White traditions found along the Eastern seaboard. In New England, there is a stronger sense of continuity with British culture, and so the ballads have remained purer, and more recognizable as being imports from the

The Irish band Reel Union. PHOTO COURTESY: Green Linnet Records.

old world. The New Englanders have also preserved a special group of songs called sea shanteys. These songs were sung by sailing men as they worked on the great sailboats and steamships, either in war or as crewmen on whaling boats.

The sea shanteys are short songs with a strong sense of rhythm. A leader would usually sing the verses, that might be connected or might simply be stray verses from many different songs, and everyone would join in either on a chorus or in a short response. The response line would be sung as a large capstan (or wheel) was turned, in order to lift an anchor, or as ropes were pulled to hoist sails. The songs helped the work go easier. Although today when we hear sea shanteys they are sung at a brisk pace, originally they were sung quite slowly. If you're hoisting a heavy anchor, you can't move too quickly!

In the South, the songs have changed more from their British forebears. There has been closer association with the musical traditions Blacks from Africa brought to the U.S. as slaves. Melodies, rhythms, and singing styles from the African continent have had a strong influence on the British songs. To me, the southern singers seem to take a more dynamic approach to the tradition, freely making changes in words, music, or rhythm, as they see fit.

Continuity and Change

After the first wave of immigration to this country ended, and the Revolutionary War was over, people began to settle in to life in America. There were many influences through the 19th and early 20th centuries that would bring change to the music of the original settlers. Although there was continuity (or a link to the past), there was also innovation, or a new American approach to old traditions.

Originally, ballads and songs were sung unaccompanied by any musical instrument. The melodies of the songs were usually based on modes, rather than the modern scales. Common folk modes use only five notes (and so are called *pentatonic*, from the Greek "penta" meaning five, and "tonic" meaning tone; see chapter 2). When people sang together, everyone sang the same melody.

Two trends worked to change the ancient modal melodies into modern melodies based on scales: one was the travelling singing masters, who brought, via the church, harmony singing to the smallest towns, and the second was the introduction of musical instruments, particularly the guitar.

In the early years of the 19th century, a religious revival swept through America, particularly among Methodists and Baptists.

Tent meetings were held where large groups of people were baptized, becoming members of the church. At these meetings, hymns were sung in an entirely new fashion. Singing masters introduced harmony singing to people who could not read music by using music books printed with different shaped notes. Each shape corresponded to a different note of the scale, so that when you saw a triangle, a diamond, or a square, you knew immediately which note to sing, even though you couldn't read music.

Although harmony singing and church melodies helped smooth out the many irregular, unusual melodies that were originally found in the Southern mountains, the Southerners also added their own unique style to church singing. The nasal, intense sounds that were always part of the Southern singing style were now made a part of church harmonizing. The high tenor part would often soar above the rest of the congregation, with a piercing clarity that could only be produced by singers long used to producing powerful, intense tones. Church harmony has influenced more recent country and bluegrass harmonizers, who also strive to achieve what some have described as a "high, lonesome sound." The singing is high in pitch and lonesome or sad in feeling.

The second major factor in the change from ancient, modal melodies to modern scales was the introduction of the guitar. From the 1850s onward, inexpensive guitars were commonly available through mail-order chains such as Sears, Roebuck and Montgomery Ward. Isolated mountaineers and small-town dwellers could send five dollars through the mail to buy a guitar. The first thing a beginning guitarist learns are three basic chords: They are known as the I-IV-V_7 chords. This simple progression can be used to accompany hundreds of songs, as long as any unusual notes are smoothed out. When singers tried to accompany themselves with the guitar, they unconsciously smoothed out the melodies that they had known and loved so that these melodies would fit the I-IV-V_7 pattern.

Singing with accompaniment makes for many changes in a song. An unaccompanied singer can pause dramatically to emphasize a certain part of text, or can vary the speed of his or her singing from verse to verse. As soon as you begin to play the guitar, the regular rhythm of the strumming tends to make you sing more evenly.

Dance Music, Musical Instruments, and the String Band

British dance music has had a large impact on American music, particularly the music for social dancing. The reel is the most

Lon Allen and son playing "The Arkansas Traveller" on 2 fiddles. PHOTOGRAPH: Russell Lee. Near Iron River, MI, 1937. Reproduction from the Collections of the Library of Congress.

common type of melody played in both North and South; in the South, a reel is often called a breakdown or hoedown tune. New England fiddlers have preserved the English, Irish, and Scottish dance traditions, playing reels, jigs, and strathspeys, as well as polkas and waltzes, originally Eastern European dances that were imported to this country through the English traditions. The Southerners have focussed most of their energy on developing a strong tradition of playing fast-paced reels in groups of fiddles, banjos, and guitars.

Musical Instruments

We have already discussed how the guitar was introduced into folk communities, and the impact that it had on folk song. Two other instruments have played an important role in American folk music: the fiddle and the banjo.

The fiddle is an imported instrument from Great Britain. American fiddle players originally played in a similar style and drew on a similar repertory of tunes as did their British forebears. Soon, however, a new style of fiddle playing developed, particularly in the South, along with a new repertory. American fiddlers tend to play with a stronger sense of rhythm than their British cousins. Emphasis is placed on bowing, and on the different sounds produced by handling the bow in different ways. The melodies have become simpler, while the execution (or how the melodies are played) has become more complex. Southern fiddlers have borrowed from African musicians a sense of syncopation, or emphasizing the off-beat.

The banjo is a native American instrument. Some musicologists believe that it is based on an African instrument, called the *banjar*. However, while there are African instruments with skin heads, the banjo is quite different in that it features a neck and fingerboard that is clearly inspired by European instruments, such as the violin and the guitar. The banjo takes an African idea and weds it to a European design. Banjo music also combines the best of African syncopation with European melody.

The banjo consists of a frame hoop, or circle, covered with a skin head. The strings pass over a bridge, or small support, that sits on the head. The vibrating bridge sets the head into vibration; the body of the instrument below the head serves as a resonator to amplify this sound. The strings pass over a neck, to tuning pegs that are used to change the pitch of the strings.

The modern banjo developed from the mid-19th century through the early years of the 20th century. An important innovation was introduced sometime in the 1850s: a shorter, "drone" string, that ran only part way up the neck, was added. This string was not usually fretted, but struck with the thumb of the right (or playing) hand, to add a constant, unchanging tone to the basic melody (called a drone, like the drone on a bagpipe). In *clawhammer* or frailing-style banjo playing, the most common older style, the playing hand is held in a loose fist or claw-like grip. The thumb catches on the drone string, while the second and third fingers brush across the melody strings.

Other popular instruments include two instruments called dulcimers, although neither instrument is related to the other. The mountain or lap dulcimer comes originally from the Scandinavian region of Europe. It is a zither; the strings of the instrument run parallel to the entire length of its body. Lap dulcimers usually have three or four strings. Two strings are never fretted; they serve as drones. The third (and fourth) strings are melody strings. They are fretted either with the left hand or with a special stick, called a *noter*. By running the hand or the noter up and down the neck, the player can produce all of the notes of the scale. The dulcimer's strings are usually vigorously strummed with the fingers, a bird's feather, or a pick. Kentucky folksinger Jean Ritchie (1922–   ) has popularized the mountain dulcimer; it has long been popular in the mountains as an ideal accompaniment for ballads and songs.

The other type of dulcimer is called a hammer dulcimer. This instrument dates back to Biblical times, and is found in Hungary, Iran, China, and Europe, in various different forms. It is also a zither; the strings run across the body of the instrument. The player strikes the strings with two small wooden mallets, or occasionally

Jeeter Gentry (banjo), Elmer Thompson
(guitar), and Fiddlin' Bill Henseley.
Asheville, North Carolina, 1937.
PHOTOGRAPH: Ben Shahn. Reproduction
from the Collections of the Library
of Congress.

will pluck the strings with the fingers. Hammer dulcimers are found
in isolated regions in Ireland, the Southern U.S., and upstate New
York, Michigan, and the Great Lakes region.

String Band Music

The introduction of the guitar and banjo into Southern music
led to a unique development: the string band. No one is quite sure
how this came about, although some believe that the first bands
consisted of two members, a fiddle player and a banjo player.
Sometime in the mid-19th century, banjo players developed a style
that was perfectly suited to accompanying the fiddle. This consisted
of playing an accompaniment that was based on the melody, rather
than only chords. The banjo player created a complementary part,
consisting of snippets of the melody played by the fiddler, some
countermelodies, and occasionally some chords. The complex in-
terplay between the two instruments is one of the most exciting
elements of string band music.

Guitar players must have come on board within a few years after
the first string bands were formed. Guitarists would either play
melody lines and chords, or simply chords. Again, because the
guitar is a chord-oriented instrument, older modal melodies would
not fit as well to guitar accompaniment. Talented guitarists ex-
perimented with different accompaniments to accomodate the unusual twists and turns of traditional dance tunes; less talented
guitarists either played chords that didn't fit the melody, or forced
the fiddle-banjo pair to alter their melody to fit the guitar chords.
In either case, the guitar had a large impact on country dance music.

Informal string bands consisting of neighbors and friends playing together on an irregular basis gave way to formal, organized bands who played for country fairs, tent shows, husking bees or other gatherings to perform necessary community work, and even for early phonograph recordings. We'll trace the history of the string band and its impact on commercial country music in Chapter 8.

Popular Dances

Instrumental music originally was played solely to accompany dancing. In the Northeast, contra dancing was the most popular form of entertainment in communities large and small. On a Saturday night, the local town hall would fill up with just about all members of the community. The contra dance is performed in two opposing lines, and consists of figures that are carried out up and down the line. The Virginia Reel is a well-known contra dance. Again, the Northerners were preserving an English tradition more or less intact, just as they did in performing English ballads and dance music.

In the South, contras gave way to the popular square and round dances. Square dances are performed by four couples in a square formation. Round dances are performed by as many couples as can comfortably fit into a hall, with all hands joined and in a big circle. Both dances employ similar figures; you are probably familiar with many of them, including the grand right and left, do-si-do, allemand left, and so on. Square dancing was popularized in this century by Lloyd Shaw, who was one of the founders of the Western Square movement. Through his work in documenting square dancing, many clubs were formed, and today it has become one of the most popular forms of dance in the country.

R·E·A·D

Botkin, B. A., *A Treasury of American Folklore*. New York: Crown Publishers, 1944.

Jackson, George Pullen, *White Spirituals in the Southern Uplands*. Hatboro, PA: Folklore Associates, 1964.

Lomax, John A. and Alan, *American Ballads and Folk Songs*. New York: Macmillan, 1934.

Sharp, Cecil J. and Maud Karpeles, *Eighty English Folk Songs from the Southern Appalachians*. Cambridge, MA: The MIT Press, 1968.

L·I·S·T·E·N

Vocal Music

Chandler, Dillard, *End of an Old Song.* Folkways 2418
Lunsford, Bascom Lamar, *Smoky Mountain Ballads.* Folkways 2040
Riddle, Almeda, *Ballads & Hymns from the Ozarks.* Rounder 0017, 0083
Ritchie, Jean, *British Traditional Ballads in the Southern Mountains.* Folkways 2301, 2302
Various, *Brave Boys: Folk Music of New England.* New World 239
Various, *Brighten the Corner Where You Are: Religious Music.* New World 224
Various, *Fine Times at Our House (Folk Music of Indiana).* Folkways 3809
Various, *High Atmosphere.* Rounder 0028
Various, *Oh My Darling: Folk Type Songs.* New World 245
Various, *Old Love Songs of Big Laurel, NC.* Folkways 2309
Various, *Social Harp: American Shape-Note Singing.* Rounder 0094

Fiddle Music

Fraley, J. P., and Annadeene, *Wild Rose of the Mountain.* Rounder 0037
Haley, Ed, *Parkersburg Landing.* Rounder 1010
Jarrell, Tommy, *Sail Away Ladies.* County 756
Lundy, Emmett W., *Fiddle Tunes.* String 802
Various, *American Fiddle Tunes.* Library of Congress, Archive of Folksong AFS L62.
Various, *New England Traditional Fiddling.* JEMF 105
Various, *37th Old-Time Fiddler's Convention, Union Grove.* Folkways 2434

Banjo Music

Boggs, Dock. Folkways 2351
Holcomb, Roscoe, *The High, Lonesome Sound.* Folkways 2368
Jarrell, Tommy, *Banjo Album.* County 748
Kazee, Buell. June Appal 009
Steele, Pete. Folkways 3828
Various, *American Banjo.* Folkways 2314
Various, *Banjo Pickin' Girls.* Rounder 1028
Various, *Clawhapper Banjo, Vols 1, 2, 3.* County 701, 717, 757
Various, *Mountain Banjo Songs & Tunes.* County 515
Various, *Old Time Banjo in America.* Kicking Mule 204
Ward, Wade, *Memorial.* Folkways 2380

Stringbands and other Instrumental Traditions (For more listings, see Chapter 8)

Various, *Instrumental Music of the Southern Appalachians.* Tradition 1007
Various, *New England Contra Dance Music.* Kicking Mule 216
Various, *Traditional Music of Grayson & Carrol Counties, VA.* Folkways 3811

6

Black American music

The folk music of Black America is a synthesis of two ingredients: the rhythmic, vocal, and instrumental traditions of Africa with the repertory of the British settlers. This two-way street between these cultures led to the creation of what many consider to be America's only unique musical forms: ragtime, jazz, blues, and spirituals. It is unlikely that this could have happened in Europe or Africa alone, without the cross-pollination of cultures that occurred in America.

I will be drawing on many early accounts of Black musicians gathered by Eileen Southern, author of *The Music of Black Americans*. In some of these accounts, pejorative expressions are used to describe Black Americans. We must remember that these early writers were themselves biased against Black Americans, whom they only knew as slaves. We can be thankful that we live in a different era, when such hatred and misunderstanding is no longer the norm.

Coming to the New Land

The majority of Black Americans came to this country on slave ships. The slave trade began in the early 17th century, and was not abolished until the end of the Civil War. Slaves were imported to White households throughout the original 13 colonies. Although today we think of slavery as being found primarily in the Southern

U.S., during at least the first century of the slave trade there were as many slaves bought and sold in the Northern cities as there were in the Southern plantations. Most of the slaves came from the West coast of Africa, in an area extending from Senegal in the North down through Zaire (the Congo) in the South. This region was known as the "Gold Coast," although the riches it bore were primarily in human flesh.

While Black slaves continued to perform traditional African music and dance, they also began to be indoctrinated in White American music. Many slaves were taught to play the violin, flute, piano, and guitar, the popular parlor instruments of the day, by White masters who wanted entertainment as well as physical labor from their slaves. Some blacks formed quintets, string bands, and brass bands to perform for Black gatherings and their White masters.

Some slaves became so proficient at playing White musical instruments that they developed a side business in teaching other servants to play. This advertisement for a runaway slave, which appeared in the Boston *Evening Post* in 1743, warns against employing a runaway as a music teacher:

> Whereas Cambridge, a Negro Man . . . doth absent himself sometimes from his Master: said Negro plays well upon a flute . . . This is to desire all Masters and Heads of Families not to suffer said Negro to come into their Houses to teach their Prentices or Servants to play, nor on any other Accounts.

A slave with musical abilities was more valuable than merely one who was a hard worker.

Black fiddler from Harper's Ferry, VA.
PHOTOGRAPH: John H. Tarbell, 1903. Reproduction from the Collections of the Library of Congress.

Ring Shouts and Worksongs: The First Black Folk Music

African music is primarily performed by large groups, for specific religious or social functions, such as to celebrate the circumcision ceremony that introduces a young man into tribal life. There are African solo traditions, but these are less common because they demand that the musician specialize in the performance and composing of music, a luxury that few African tribes could afford. (For more information on African music, see Volume I of this series, *Man's Earliest Music*).

Life in the New World did not allow for many large-scale gatherings of Blacks. For one thing, working in the field or in a White household all day left little energy on evenings for large social gatherings. For another, White owners were not anxious to encourage Blacks to socialize. Slaves from one area of Africa might be sold up and down the Eastern Coast of America, which tended to break down tribal allegiances and ancient customs. Although some Whites were concerned with the plight of the slaves, they did not recognize the value of African culture. Instead, they tried to "civilize" the slaves by introducing them to White religion, culture, and music.

In the mid-18th century, White religious leaders in the North began a drive to convert Black slaves. One of the strongest means of introducing Blacks to the White religion was the hymns. Hymn singing allowed Black slaves to gather in groups to sing together, as they had done in Africa. It was one of the few outlets for communal singing that was allowed in North or South.

The White hymns had Western-style melodies and harmonies that were unknown in Africa. The Black slaves were quick to adapt these melodies, by bending notes, adding slides, grace notes, and ornaments, and by changing harmonies, so that the music took on a distinctly African flavor. The rhythms were also changed, from the four-square, regular marchlike tempo that the hymn writers employed, to a syncopated emphasis of the off-beat. Most striking was the vocal style used by the Black singers; they sang in an intense, powerful voice, almost shouting the words of the hymns. The shouting intensity of the singing mirrored the intensity of the feelings.

In the years from the 1780s through the 1830s, a great religious explosion occurred in the United States. Camp meetings were held where large groups of people "got religion" and joined the church. Although these meetings were segregated, often the Black participants were more vocal and enthusiastic than the Whites. The camp meetings also introduced a new form of hymn, one based on the folk melodies of traditional White songs, with verses made up of fragments from the Bible, popular songs, and poetry, interspersed with shouts of "Hallelujah" and "Amen."

Camp meetings often lasted for several days, and ran from dusk to dawn. The Black enthusiasm for religious expression would heighten as the days went by, much to the alarm of the slave owners, who were ever fearful that the Blacks would break out from under their control. The Blacks did not sit still while they sang, as did their White brethren. Instead, they often formed an impromptu circle, dancing in an exaggerated walking step, called a "shuffle" by the White slave owners. In Africa, religious expression was usually accompanied by dancing, and so it was to be in America. The *ring shout*, or hymn that was shouted and sung by a group of dancers, was the first marriage of African movements, rhythms, and singing style, with a White American musical form. Here's a description from a White author written in 1867:

> More than half the population of the plantation is gathered together . . . Old and young, men and women . . . stand up in the middle of the floor, and when the "sperichil" [spiritual] is struck up, begin first walking and by-and-by shuffling round, one after the other, in a ring. The foot is hardly taken from the floor, and the progression is mainly due to a jerking, hitching motion, which agitates the entire shoulder . . .

The "jerking" movement of the body expresses the religious "spirit" entering the body of the celebrant. The spirit literally is "with" the person who is singing. This idea of spiritual oneness is derived from African religious ceremonies.

The spiritual is a special Black adaptation of White hymns. As more Blacks were converted, those with musical talent compiled hymn books, just as White ministers had done before them. They often selected hymns with a special message for slaves: telling of the freedom that was coming in heaven, instilling hope for a better life in the other world. What sets apart the spirituals is not only their message, but the manner in which they were sung. Again, Blacks expressed more intensity in their singing, often swaying or moving to the music.

Religious music was not the only means of expression for the slaves. Another important outlet was the worksongs. The field shout had its roots in African music, but borrowed melodies and words from America. Workers would be spread out in huge fields of cotton or crops. To communicate with each other, they would shout back and forth, trading lines of a song, or casually improvising new words to a familiar tune. Sometimes, the shout would serve to communicate important messages. Huddie Ledbetter (1885-1949), better known today as the folksinger Leadbelly, recalled working in the hot summer sun. The water boy was a young slave who would bring water to the thirsty workers. Leadbelly sang this shout to attract the attention of the water boy:

> Bring me little water, Silvie,
> Bring me little water, now,
> Bring me little water, Silvie,
> Every little once in a while.

This shout was performed by chain gangs in the South, performing heavy labor, such as breaking up rocks with mallets, and so was performed very slowly, and included many pauses for the workers to lift their mallets and then to let them fall:

> Go down Ol' Hannah,
> And don't you rise no mo',
> If you rise in the mornin',
> Bring Judgment Day.
> Huh!

Many of the worksongs were performed in a call-and-response style. This is commonly found in Africa, as well as in White American hymns. In call-and-response, the leader or main vocalist sings one line of the melody (or an entire verse), and then the entire group responds with either another line or a chorus. The call-and-response form is perfect for worksongs, because it allows one leader to set a rhythm and pace for the job to be done. Leadbelly was famous on plantations and chain gangs as an excellent and tireless worker and song leader.

Mance Lipscomb. PHOTOGRAPH: Chris Strachwitz.
PHOTO COURTESY: Arhoolie Records.

Dance Music and Playparties

The Black slaves quickly adopted the favorite White musical instrument to accompany their own social dances: the fiddle. Black fiddlers were soon in demand at gatherings of Blacks and Whites alike. The country dances that were imported from England became favorites of Black performers. While they performed the same figures as their White masters, they introduced new rhythmic steps that were to lead to the creation of several unique American dance forms: clogging, step dancing, and ultimately tap dancing.

The musical capability of many Black musicians and callers amazed White authors, who often described them as possessing superhuman abilities, playing into the myth that Blacks were a special species of humans who were perhaps half devil:

> Old Frank Johnson's (Negro) String Band furnished the music and who ever heard better dance music than this? It is said that, as the night wore away, this remarkably gifted [fiddler] has often been known to lose consciousness and go to sleep, yet go on calling figures and never make a mistake.

Fiddle and banjo both were called "devil's instruments" by those who wished to suppress the energetic playing of Black and White musicians alike. Stories like this one supported that myth.

Along with fiddle music, Blacks performed many songs merely for fun. Young people would gather together to husk corn, roll logs, raise a roof, or any other event that involved both manpower and a good excuse to bring the neighborhood together. Often this was the only chance for young people to become romantically involved, as there were few opportunities for courtship. At these meetings, nonsense songs consisting of many different floating verses were performed. A floating verse is one that is found in many different songs, and can be freely inserted or deleted into any context. The songs don't tell a story, but rather relate a mood. Many of these songs have been recorded from both Blacks and Whites, such as "Black-Eyed Susie":

> Harpers creek and roaring river,
> There my dear we'll live together.
>
> CHORUS: Hey, hey, Black-eyed Susie,
> I'm going to marry Black-eyed Susie.
>
> Up the creek and down salt water
> Some old fella stole my daughter.
>
> All I want in this creation,
> Pretty little wife and a big plantation.
>
> All I want to make me happy,
> Two little boys to call me pappy.

The Blues

The Civil War led to the "freeing" of all slaves. However, many slaves were unable to leave the large Southern plantations, lacking the resources to purchase their own farms. Many remained working on the large farms, as sharecroppers. In effect, although they were supposed to share in the profits of the plantation, they remained enslaved. Freedom did allow some Blacks to take to the roads, to try to find work in the cities, move out into the unsettled lands of the West, or to take up a life of panhandling, scraping together income by performing odd jobs, working as field hands during the harvest time, and, for some, performing as street musicians.

After the Civil War, an important new instrument was introduced into the countryside: the guitar. We have already described (in Chapter 5) how the guitar changed White music, introducing modern harmonies and rhythms. The guitar also had a large impact on Black music, although Black guitarists were able to preserve their own sense of scale, rhythm, and harmony.

Larry Sandberg and Dick Weissman, in *The Folk Music Sourcebook*, describe how Black guitarists were able to shape a unique accompaniment style that enabled them to continue to sing their songs using many flattened notes, vocal slides, and syncopated rhythms. The guitar echoed the voice of the singer; it became another voice. Just as in call-and-response, where a leader sings a line and then the group responds, blues singers will sing a line of the verse and then let the guitar "answer" by playing a melodic line.

Blues guitarists "bend" notes when they play the guitar by pushing against the strings with the fingers of their fretting hand, thus

Black Minstrel Banjo Player, c. 1890s.
Reproduction from the Collections of
the Library of Congress.

changing the pitch of the note. This technique enables them to play many quarter and half tones that lie between the notes of the scale. Some Black guitarists developed a technique using a glass bar (such as the neck of a bottle) or a piece of metal, sliding it up and down the neck of the guitar. This allows them to play many more notes than those you can produce by pressing down the strings at the frets. Black guitarists also use different tunings to allow for different harmonic accompaniments.

The classic blues structure is called the twelve bar blues. In the twelve-bar form, the singer sings and plays three melodic phrases, each four bars long. The first and second line are the same:

Got the blues, can't be satisfied
Got the blues, can't be satisfied
Reason why, I hangs my head and cries.

Although each melodic phrase lasts for four bars (or 16 beats), in many blues songs the words might only last for as little as nine beats; this leaves a large "gap" in the lyrics. This space is filled by playing melodic lines on the guitar. Sometimes, a singer will simply drop part of the words to allow the guitar to "sing" the rest of the words. Or, sometimes the vocal line will last a full four bars, and then the musician will insert a "fill" or short instrumental part that extends the length of the entire blues.

The origin of the blues form is unknown. By the end of the 19th century, there were many different blues styles that were being played throughout the South. The Mississippi delta area produced an intense, highly charged style of performance. Many of these blues guitarists played for dances or in saloons, in whorehouses, or on the streets, wherever they could pick up some extra change. The Delta blues, as they are known today, described the dark underside of life among gamblers, pimps, and prostitutes. The guitarists played many slow blues, letting the guitar take the place of the vocalist and "sing," and using the metal or glass slide and special tunings to produce the melodies. Famous Delta bluesmen include Robert Johnson (c. 1912-1937) and Son House.

In the middle South, a more light-hearted blues was performed. This is sometimes called ragtime-blues, because of its syncopated melodies. The guitarists picked the strings with their fingers. The thumb would establish a regular bass on the lower strings of the guitar. The second and third fingers would pick a melody that emphasized the off-beats. By placing these syncopated melody lines against the regular bass beat, the guitarist created an effect not unlike ragtime pianists. Most of these ragtime blues songs consisted of verses that expressed a more rosy outlook on life than did the Delta blues. Often, they consisted of floating verses taken from playparty songs that were sung for comic effect. Famous ragtime

Jimmie Strothers (guitar) and Joe Lee
(vocal) perform "Do Lord Remember Me."
Virginia State Convict Farm, 1936.
Reproduction from the Collections of the
Library of Congress.

blues performers include the Reverend Gary Davis (1894-1972),
Elizabeth Cotten (c. 1900-   ), and Pink Anderson.

Another popular blues form joined words about religious experiences with a blues guitar accompaniment. These religious blues
were related to the spirituals and ring shouts that came before
them. The singer often shouted the lyrics, to express his or her
deep conviction. The difference was that the lyrics were now set
to blues guitar accompaniments. In this way, religious singers were
able to reach a wider audience, because of the popularity of the
country blues.

The country blues were brought to urban audiences as Blacks
migrated from the country to the city. At the turn of the century,
"The Memphis Blues" was a hit, and it made composer W. (William) C. (Christopher) Handy (1873-1958) famous. Handy, a
trained musician, made the blues attractive to a city audience by
smoothing out its irregularities, and adapting the blues to the dance-
band format. He was later to call himself the "Father of the Blues."

After World War II, a new development came that changed the
blues from a solo guitar tradition into something new. The introduction of the electric guitar enabled bluesmen to perform in noisy
bars. A large number of Blacks in urban areas, particularly in
Chicago, made up a ready audience for this music. The result was
city or electric blues. The guitarist was joined by a group usually
including a harmonica (or harp) player, perhaps a pianist, and a
drummer. The guitarist was freed from playing both melody and
accompaniment to focussing on melody alone. Famous city bluesmen include Muddy Waters (McKinley Morganfield, 1915-1980)
and B.B. King (1925-   ).

Ragtime and Jazz

Black folk music had a profound impact on two Black musical forms that are today considered to be Black America's classical music: ragtime and jazz. Ragtime piano developed at about the same time as the blues. Pianos were not readily available to Blacks, so they had to go to places that had pianos. In church, a lucky few could learn to play the organ. In a saloon or whorehouse, a piano was usually kept on hand to provide entertainment. Those who were fortunate enough to attend one of the Black colleges or secondary schools that had a good music department could learn the rudiments of performance there.

Scott Joplin (1868-1917) is the best-known ragtime pianist and composer today. He wrote the best-selling ragtime piece of all time, "The Maple Leaf Rag." He studied music theory and piano playing as a boy in Texarkana, Texas, and then as a teenager travelled up the Mississippi in search of employment. He came to St. Louis in 1885, and soon was playing in local saloons and composing marches, popular songs, and piano pieces all in the style typical of that era, while also performing the occasional rag. Joplin was a jack-of-all-trades when it came to music, forming his own vocal octet (group of eight singers) to tour through the Midwest. In 1899, he met a local furniture dealer who had ambitions to be a music publisher. John Stark became a champion not only of Joplin's work but of all Black-composed ragtime. He was one of the few White publishers who did not edit the music to make it easier to play.

While ragtime was developing, another trend was leading to the creation of jazz. Brass bands were formed by Blacks throughout the South, as a means of gaining employment playing for local town functions and at the occasional funeral. In the New Orleans area, the brass bands began to perform syncopated versions of popular White marches. This syncopated music attracted the attention of both Blacks and Whites. Soon, syncopated bands were in demand for dances throughout the country, and jazz was born. Jazz has gone through many changes over the last 80 years, as both Black and White musicians from classical, folk, and popular backgrounds have added new instruments and styles of playing to the jazz repertory.

R·E·A·D

Bastin, Bruce, *Cryin' for the Carolines*. London: Studio Vista, 1971.

Charters, Samuel, *The Bluesmen*. New York: Oak Publications, 1967.

Charters, Samuel, *The Country Blues*. New York: Da Capo Press, 1959.

Courlander, Harold, *Negro Folk Music USA*. New York: Columbia University Press, 1963.

Guralnick, Peter, *Feel Like Going Home*. New York: E. P. Dutton, 1971.

Heilbut, Tony, *The Gospel Sound*. New York: Simon & Schuster, 1971.

Jackson, Bruce, *Wake Up Dead Man*. Cambridge, MA: Harvard University Press, 1972.

Jones, Bessie and Bess Lomax Hawes, *Step it Down*. New York: Harper & Row, 1972.

Jones, Leroi, *Blues People*. New York: Morrow, 1963.

Lomax, John and Alan, *Negro Folk Songs as Sung by Leadbelly*. New York: Macmillan, 1936.

Neff, Robert, and Anthony Connor, *Blues*. Boston, MA: David R. Godine, 1975.

Oliver, Paul, *The Story of the Blues*. New York: Chilton, 1969.

Ramsey, Frederic Jr., *Been Here and Gone*. New Brunswick, NJ: Rutgers University Press, 1969.

Rooney, James, *Bossmen: Bill Monroe and Muddy Waters*. New York: Dial Press, 1971.

Southern, Eileen, *The Music of Black Americans; A History*. New York: W. W. Norton, 1971.

 L·I·S·T·E·N

Anthologies and Overviews

Various, *Been in the Storm So Long*. Folkways 3842

Various, *Georgia Sea Islands Songs*. New World 278

Various, *God Give Me Light*. Herwin 203

Various, *Jugs, Jook, & Washboard Bands*. Blues Classics 2

Various, *Library of Congress Field Recordings, Texas 1934-39*. Herwin 211

Various, *Music of the South, Vols. 1-10*. Folkways 2650-59

Various, *Negro Prison Songs*. Tradition 1020

Various, *Ragtime in Rural America*. New World 235

Various, *Roots of the Blues*. New World 252

Various, *Wake Up Dead Man*. Rounder 2013

Blues

Blake, Blind, *Vol. 1, 2, 3, 4, 5.* Biograph 12003, 12023, 12031, 12037, 12050
Carter, Bo, *Greatest Hits.* Yazoo 1014
Cotten, Elizabeth, *Folk Songs.* Folkways 3526
Davis, Reverend Gary, *In Concert.* Kicking Mule 101
Fuller, Blind Boy, *1935–1942.* Blues Classics 11
House, Son, *Library of Congress Recordings.* Folk Lyric 9002
Hurt, Mississippi John, *1928 Sessions.* Yazoo 1065
James, Skip. Biograph 12029
Jefferson, Blind Lemon, *Vol. 1, 2.* Biograph 12000, 12015
Johnson, Blind Willie. Yazoo 1058
Leadbelly, *Last Sessions.* Folkways 2941, 2942
McTell, Blind Willie, *Vols. 1 & 2.* Yazoo 1005, 1037
Patton, Charlie. Yazoo 1020
Taylor, Hound Dog, and the Houserockers. Alligator 4702
Taylor, Koko, *From the Heart of a Woman.* Alligator 4724
Various, *Blues Roots/Mississippi.* RBF 14
Various, *Country Blues.* RBF 1, 9
Various, *Country Blues Classics, Vols. 1-4.* Blues Classics 5, 6, 7, 14
Various, *Delta Blues.* Herwin 214
Various, *Georgia Blues.* Rounder 2008
Various, *Let's Get Loose.* New World 290
Various, *Mississippi Blues.* Yazoo 1001
Various, *Mississippi Delta Blues, Vols. 1 & 2.* Arhoolie 1041, 1042
Various, *South Mississippi Blues.* Rounder 2009
Various, *The Rural Blues.* RBF 202
Various, *When Women Sang the Blues.* Blues Classics 26

Immigrant and ethnic music

7

The United States is often called a "nation of immigrants." The founding fathers (and mothers) of this country came to the U.S. to escape religious persecution in Europe; they were determined to establish a nation where everyone could have the freedom to follow their own beliefs. Although there have been periods in American history when racial bigotry and prejudice have dominated the politics of the moment, in general we have been one of the few nations to extend open arms to the suffering and impoverished of the world. Today, America has one of the most diverse populations on the globe. Moreover, the second, third, and fourth generations of these immigrants no longer think of themselves as first and foremost Germans, Slavs, Italians, English, Greeks, Cubans, or Jews: They think of themselves as Americans. In many other countries where different groups live together, friction, dissent, and violence frequently occur.

In this chapter, we'll examine just a few of the rich musical traditions that made the trip from Europe to the New World. First, we'll take a look at two traditions that come from closer to home: the Louisiana French traditions of Cajun and Zydeco music, and the Tex-Mex border music. Then, we'll turn our attention to Irish, Jewish, and Scandinavian traditions.

The Historical Background

From the first decades of the 19th century through the end of the 1920s, new groups of immigrants came to the United States. Not all were happy to be leaving their homes, but most were faced with

French, African, Spanish, and American idioms. Cajun music is performed by the descendants of the White, French settlers, and is strongly influenced by French, Anglo-American, and Black instrumental traditions. Zydeco (sometimes called *zodico*) is the music promise of health, wealth, and new opportunities in the New World.

It is not uncommon for modern Americans to take a vacation in Europe, travelling by air and reaching their destination in a matter of hours. It is hard to realize the magnitude of the journey that the immigrants made. The trip by sea from Liverpool (the port of exit from England) to the United States could take up to three months; the trip to Liverpool (from all corners of Europe) might take as long. Later in the 19th century, steamships and railroads made travel easier, but a trip across Europe was still a fairly large undertaking. Sometimes, an immigrant had to raise money as he or she went along, taking several months at any one stop in order to earn the capital for the next leg of the trip.

Modern telephone, mail, and telegraph networks make communicating across the globe simple; in the early days of world communication, it was not unusual for letters to take months to make the crossing, and for many items to be lost. When a father left his family in Europe, promising to write home and (eventually) to send enough money so that they could follow, it was not always certain that they would ever see or hear from him again.

Why did ordinary, poor, working people make the decision to leave their homes? For most, the world was changing rapidly around them. Most of the lower classes in Europe worked on small farms; they depended on their own physical labor—and factors beyond their control such as the success of a year's crops, weather, and the health of family members who worked the soil—in order to make a living. In many parts of Europe, industrialization was spelling the end of the family or communal farm. Machines were replacing workers. Traditionally hand-made items, such as clothing or shoes, were now being made by machine. The spread of industrialization moved steadily from England (at the turn of the 18th century) through Germany (midcentury) to Italy, Poland, and Eastern Europe (end of the century). Natural disasters had their own special impact on the flood of immigration; most famous was the Irish potato famine of 1845, which destroyed most of this important food crop, leading to mass starvation and a huge exodus of rural Irish poor from their homeland to this country.

The impact of immigration on the United States can be appreciated by comparing the growth of population in the entire country from 1820 to 1930 to the numbers of immigrants who

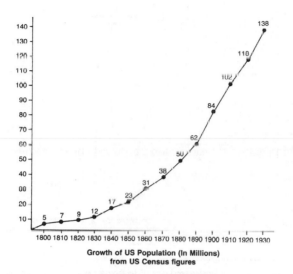

**Growth of US Population (In Millions)
from US Census figures**

came here in the same period. I have sketched two graphs that show this growth in simplified form.

In 1800, the United States had just emerged from the war of independence to being a small independent nation of approximately 5 million people, mostly living on the Eastern seaboard. Growth was slow from 1800–1820, with the population almost doubling in size. By 1840, the population had nearly doubled again, but was still a small 17 million. In the period from 1840 to the turn of the century, the population grew sharply, to reach 84 million. Then, another spurt came that pushed the population, in the next 30 years, to a high of 138 million, or approximately 50 million more people. Some of this growth was due to improved medical care and a growing birth rate. However, a good part of this growth was due to the influx of immigrants, a total of 35 million people over a 100-year period beginning in 1830.

Historian Oscar Handlin has divided this period into three waves of immigration. During the first wave, from approximately 1815 (the end of the War of 1812) to 1860 (the beginning of the Civil War), immigrants from England, Ireland, and Germany travelled to this country, with the Irish and German immigration coming toward the end of the period. The biggest influx of Irish came in the 10 years following the potato famine, which pushed immigration from 84,000 people in 1830 up to a high point of 427,000 in 1854. The outbreak of the Civil War made travel to the U.S. difficult, ending this first wave.

The second wave of immigration began at war's end, when new laws were passed encouraging workers to come to the United States.

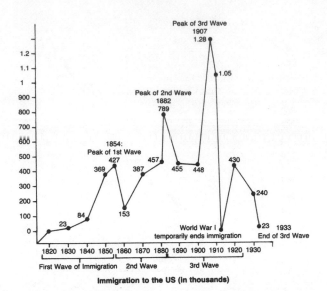

Immigration to the US (in thousands)

circumstances that made conditions at home intolerable. For them, the long and dangerous trip to the United States was worth the risk, when balanced against the changing world at home and the

Around the turn of the century, new social forces in Europe created the third wave of immigration. Religious groups, such as the Eastern European Jews, were suffering oppression at the hands of political leaders who conducted massive purges of people whom they considered to be "undesirable." This wave crested in 1907, when approximately 1.28 million people came to America.

The outbreak of World War I in 1914 closed off all ports of entry to immigrants for a period of four years. Following the war, immigration shot up to 430,000, but soon dropped off. In the Depression years of the 1930s, immigration was down to 23,000, as low as it had been a 100 years previously.

The immigrants came to this country with a rich heritage of music, dance, and culture. Many settled in tightly knit communities. Some lived on the same blocks in urban areas, quickly establishing native-language newspapers, theaters, and clubs. Others moved to small farming towns in the Midwest; large numbers of Scandinavians, for instance, chose to follow a life of farming in Minnesota. Although they lived on large farms in fairly islolated spots, they kept in touch with their neighbors, who usually hailed from the same part of Europe as they did.

Record companies recognized in the immigrants a new market for their product: phonographs and records. Columbia records even published special instructions to their sales forces on how to exploit this new audience:

With between five and eight thousand miles between them and the land of their birth, in a country of strange speech and customs, the 35 million foreigners making their home here are keenly on the alert for anything and everything which will keep alive the memories of the fatherland. . . . It is easy to realize why the talking machine appeals to them so potently . . . If you are not getting your share of it, you are overlooking a large and profitable business which, moreover, is right at your door . . .

Despite the crass commercialism of the record companies, they did perform a valuable service by preserving many of the popular immigrant musicians, singers, and bands on records. Without these recordings, we would know little today about this music.

Cajun and Zydeco Music

In the 16th, 17th, and 18th centuries, three major powers fought for control of the American continent: Spain, France, and England. We speak English today and carry on many British traditions because the English were victorious. However, there are parts of the country where the influence of the two other cultures remain strong. One area is the Louisiana bayou country, where many different cultures have come together to form two related musical styles: *cajun* and *zydeco* music.

The Cajuns are descendants of the French Acadians who originally settled in Nova Scotia around 1600. British settlers fought with the French for a little over a century, finally driving all of the French settlers out. Homesick for French culture, they eventually worked their way down to "New France," a French stronghold in an area that is now part of Louisiana. Many settled in the swampy farmlands around New Orleans, known as the Louisiana bayou. They established small farms, while also living off of the abundant fish and wildlife in the swamps.

Two other groups were already present in this area. One was native Indians, who lived in small groups scattered throughout the area. The other was Black slaves, who were brought in large numbers to Louisiana by wealthy White landowners who needed cheap labor. The Louisiana Blacks preserved a rich African heritage, including elaborate dance rituals accompanied by African-style drums, for many years longer than Blacks settled in other parts of the country (See Chapter 6). The Spanish influence was also felt, because Louisiana is close to the Mexican border, and other immigrant groups, particularly Germans and Scotch-Irish, had an impact on the musical culture that developed.

These groups freely mixed in bayou and town. The Cajun language, originally a dialect of French, became a distinct mix of

This wave crested in 1882, when 789,000 immigrants came to this country. At this time, American workers began to worry that they would be unable to compete with immigrants who were willing to work longer hours, for less pay. New laws were passed to make immigration more difficult, and in the following 20 years, immigration dropped off.

performed by the Creole peoples of the region, who have Black, Indian, and Spanish blood in their veins.

Both Cajun and Zydeco musics are played primarily to accompany dances, with snatches of verses sung to the tunes. The verses "float" from song to song, and usually concern themselves with lost love. Some have been borrowed from popular songs, particularly the sentimental songs that were popular throughout the South in the late 19th century. From the French and English traditions, the Cajuns have picked up a strong sense of melody; from the Black-African traditions, they have gained a unique sense of syncopated rhythm. From Southern country music, the Cajuns have learned a vocal style that emphasizes the higher end of the vocal range, and a lonesome, nasal sound. Zydeco music, being closer to the Black tradition, is more melodic and less lyrically oriented, as you might expect.

The lead instrument in both Cajun and Zydeco traditions comes from neither Black nor English roots. It is the German diatonic

Black accordion and Washboard player. New Iberia, Louisiana. PHOTOGRAPH: Russell Lee. Reproduction from the Collections of the Library of Congress.

melodian (a member of the accordion family). Because melodians are inexpensive and loud, they are the ideal instrument to play in large dance halls. The classic Cajun band features melodian, fiddle, and triangle (as percussion). The guitar came in fairly early as well, replaced now by electric guitar and bass to provide rhythm. Drums are common in modern bands.

The most famous Cajun performers are the Balfa Brothers' band (accordion, fiddle, and guitar) and, in the younger generation, Marc Savoy (accordion player and builder). In Zydeco, Clifton Chenier (piano accordion) has had the most success, performing a mixture of energetic dance music and plaintive blues.

Tex-Mex Music

A little further West from Louisiana's bayou country is the Texas-Mexican border, where another unique musical style has developed. This music is popularly known as "Tex-Mex" music, because it combines the country music of Texas with the Spanish-influence of Mexican music. As in Cajun country, other ethnic groups have had a hand in forming this style, particularly the Germans.

Tex-Mex dance music is played in bands usually featuring accordion, guitar, bass, and drums, with a strong vocal tradition. Two of the most popular instrumentalists are Santiago and Flaco Jiminez, father-and-son masters of the accordion. Another important aspect of the Tex-Mex tradition is the lyric song. The Spanish *corrido* is a long story-song that tells about local events, the courtship of two lovers, or even national or international events. These songs can be accompanied by an entire band, or by a solo guitar. Lydia Mendoza gained fame singing *corridos* in the 1920s, thanks to her recordings with her family and as a soloist. Her fine voice and excellent repertory of songs made her a great star.

In the past, Tex-Mex musicians had to hide their ethnic identity in order to break into pop music. Freddy Fender, the singer/songwriter whose "Before the Next Teardrop Falls" was a country hit in 1975, was born Baldemar Huerta. "It's much easier for a gringo [White American] to drop a dime in the juke if the artist's name is Freddy Fender," he commented about his name change. Prejudice against Mexican performers sadly continues today.

Eire in the New World: Music of the Irish Immigrants

The Irish were among the first to emigrate to America, with large numbers coming beginning in 1845 after the potato famine. They played a key role in fighting the Civil War, building the nation's railroads, mining coal and settling farms, working in America's largest cities, and eventually entering American political life as policemen, mayors, and Congressmen; one particularly successful Irish politician became this country's 35th president, John Fitzgerald Kennedy.

When the Irish originally came to this country, many less-than-enlightened employers ended their job solicitations with the line "NO IRISH NEED APPLY." The "No-Nothing" movement was made up of groups of American Protestants who were afraid that large numbers of Irish Catholics would flood the country, taking away jobs and replacing the American President with the Pope. This blind hatred dominated American life for many years; when John F. Kennedy ran for President, it reared its head again, when reporters asked Kennedy whether he would keep his first allegiance to the country or the Catholic Church. Fortunately, these prejudices are forgotten in most parts of America.

The Irish have always been proud of their heritage. Young Irish-American children are encouraged to take lessons in Gaelic (the traditional language of Ireland), step dancing, and music. To appreciate the impact of the Irish on American life, let's look at just one city: Chicago.

By 1850, only five years after the potato famine began, 20 percent of Chicago's population was Irish. The Irish initially settled in neighborhoods that were cut off from other ethnic groups in the

Los Pinguinos del Norte.
PHOTOGRAPH: Chris Strachwitz. PHOTO COURTESY: Arhoolie Records.

city, mostly in slums near the city's industrial core, where meat, lumber, grain, and bricks were processed and shipped throughout the country. The smell of slaughtered meat, the noise of heavy machinery, the constant movement of horse-drawn wagons, and the sounds of steam locomotives were all a part of the everyday life of these families. The names of Irish neighborhoods mixed traditional Irish family names with descriptive words that give a flavor of what life was like in these areas: Conley's Patch, Healy's Slough [mudhole or ditch], and the Back o' the Yards.

The Irish did not remain on the bottom of the social ladder for long. Soon, they were taking positions of responsibility at work and in city government. One Irishman, Francis James O'Neill rose to be Chief of Police in Chicago, after serving for many years as a Captain. Happily for the future history of Irish music, he was also a flutist and interested in preserving Irish music and dance. He formed the Chicago Irish Music Club, and encouraged the best musicians to stay in Chicago by providing steady work for them as members of the police force! O'Neill published many collections of Irish dance music; his *The Music of Ireland* (1,850 tunes, published in 1903) has become a standard collection of Irish dance music.

With better jobs came better income. The Irish were able to move out of the poorest neighborhoods, some to working-class neighborhoods in town, some to the more exclusive suburbs. In the 1920s, many, including O'Neill, lamented that Irish culture would die if the Irish were totally assimilated (or drawn into) American life. However, dance bands and dancing schools flourished. In New York City, there was a dance hall named for every province in Ireland (35 in all)! Many of the greatest Irish musicians of the day made good livings by augmenting day jobs with making records and performing for dances and social events. Michael Coleman, a master fiddler originally from County Sligo in Ireland, had an exclusive contract with Columbia records, which meant that he was paid a certain amount of money whether he recorded or not!

The musical instruments traditionally played in Ireland—fiddle, pipes, and flute—came with the immigrants to America. In this country, new instruments became part of the tradition. The guitar became a popular accompaniment instrument, as well as the piano. Mandolins, tenor banjos, accordions, and other modern instruments also became a part of the tradition.

Today, a revival of interest in Irish music and culture has led to several small record companies being formed, competitions and festivals being held, and a renewed sense of pride in the Irish neighbors themselves.

The Klezmorim.
PHOTO COURTESY:
Flying Fish Records.

Out of Eastern Europe: Jewish Music

Throughout the 19th century, anti-Jewish movements grew in Eastern Europe. Many Jews fled their native towns, after witnessing the persecution and death of relatives and friends. They came to America in search of freedom, just as many generations of immigrants had done before them. They brought with them a rich musical culture.

The music of the Eastern European Jews was performed by wandering, professional musicians known as *klezmorim*; klezmer music takes its name from the Hebrew words, "klei zemer," meaning musical instruments. The klezmer performed for both Jewish and non-Jewish audiences, playing a mix of traditional Jewish and Eastern European dance tunes, contemplative slow airs, and songs.

The klezmer borrowed musical instruments from their neighbors. The original klezmer bands were probably made up of strings, particularly fiddles, cellos, and the tsimbl, a stringed zither that is played with small hammers, (a relative of the American hammer dulcimer and the Hungarian *cimbalum*). Later, when Jews were forced to join local Army brigades, they were introduced to brass instruments, flutes, clarinets, and other instruments found in the military band. Soon, these became a part of the klezmer orchestra.

The repertory of the klezmer band was a diverse mix of Yiddish dance music and song and music from the surrounding cultures. The most common dance was the *frelekh* (which means "lively"). Most dance music was played as part of the wedding ceremony. Weddings were elaborate affairs; here's a description from Jewish music scholar Henry Sapoznik:

Weddings, which lasted from one to two weeks, contained very specific and highly important tunes related to the ceremony. The klezmer would play tunes to escort the bride to the *khupe* (wedding canopy), under the khupe, and leading from it. There were specific dances just for the *mekhutonim* (parents of the bridal couple, such as the *broyges tants* (dance of anger and reconciliation). In addition there were various other wedding dances such as the *patsh tants* (hand-clapping dance), *mitzva tants* (blessing dance), and the *kosher tants*.

Besides dance music, the other major instrumental tradition is the *doina* or *volakhls*. These pieces are played in a nonrhythmic, "singing" style, imitating the chanting/singing of the cantor in the synagogue. The instrument's voice soars up and down the scale, exploring different nuances and textures. The Rumanian gypsy tradition also had a strong influence on this type of music.

Besides these Yiddish forms, the klezmer band had to be able to entertain their non-Jewish neighbors. A good musician and his band worked hard to please every audience, and so the klezmer played as many polkas and waltzes as they did doinas and freylekhs.

Ironically, the growth of Jewish consciousness in the 1920s through the 1940s led to a decline of interest in klezmer music, because it was considered to be the music of unlettered peasants. The kletzmorium, like gypsies, were considered to be travelling people of little or no education. Jews who settled in the U.S. wanted to preserve a more "refined" culture. This led to an emphasis on Hebrew folksongs, many of which were recently composed.

Still, klezmer artists recorded many 78 records from the birth of the recording industry. Each record label had its own klezmer band under contract: Abe Schwartz and his orchestra, working for Columbia, were among the most popular and prolific. Today, a klezmer revival—led by serveral young bands including the Klezmorim (in California), Kapelye (in New York), and the New England Conservatory Klezmer band (in Boston)—has led to new scholarship and recordings of this important music.

Norwegian Music in Minnesota

The story of the Norwegian immigrants in Minnesota and their music is similar to the story of the Irish, Jewish, Italian, German, Hungarian, and other immigrant groups. Most of the Norwegians came from small farming communities. It was rare for a person from one community to move to another town during his or her lifetime. The result was that each community developed its own dialect, music, and dance.

The trip to America changed all of this. Norwegians from many different parts of the country met on the boats coming to America, and many travelled together to Minnesota to establish their home-steads. Neighbors banded together to perform the heavy work of raising a roof or for group activities such as making a quilt or shucking the year's harvest of corn.

A key part of any group gathering was descriptively called the "kitchen sweat." A large group of people would cram into a kitchen or living room of a small farm house for an evening's dance following the day's work. Local musicians, some talented, some not so talented, would play the music, usually on a fiddle or melodian. These dances were all-night affairs, and gave lonely homesteaders a chance to court or flirt with someone who they might see only a few times a year.

The Norwegians brought with them a rich tradition of intricate dances. Most involved elaborate footwork and energetic leaps. They also brought an unusual folk instrument, the *hardanger fiddle*. This instrument features four melody strings, like a regular violin, but has an additional set of four drone strings that run through the body of the instrument. These drone strings are not bowed, but rather vibrate in sympathy with the melody or bowed strings.

The Norwegian dance traditions changed soon after their arrival in the United States. Their neighbors in the Midwest were a mix of many different groups, particularly Germans, Eastern Europeans, Swiss, and Polish. The Norwegian dances were unknown to these other groups, and would have been impossible to quickly master at an evening's dance. However, the Norwegians and other groups did share in common several social dances: polkas and schottisches, popular dances that had spread throughout Europe in the 19th century. These were far less strenuos than the traditional Norwegian dances, and appealed to the other immigrant groups and the younger generation of Norwegians as well.

Although today the Norwegians share a repertory of dances and tunes with their German and Slavic neighbors, they have maintained a distinct style of playing. The bowing style on the violin has a distinctive lilt or swing that is unlike the Eastern European traditions of heavy, march-like rhythms.

As the older dance traditions died out, so did the instrument that had accompanied them: the hardanger fiddle. It was replaced by the less-expensive, easier-to-play standard violin, and the many variations of accordions (melodians, concertinas, bandoneons) that were inexpensive and readily available in music stores and through mail-order catalogues.

Despite the pressures to change, the Norwegians, like the other ethnic groups we have discussed, have maintained a distinct culture. The fact that so many different groups have maintained their unique cultures in this country is a testimony to the success of our social structure.

R·E·A·D

Cajun and Zydeco

Daigle, Pierre, *Tears, Lore and Laughter*. LA.: Acadian Publishing Enterprises, 1972.

Post, Lauren, *Cajun Sketches*. Baton Rouge, LA: Louisiana State University Press, 1962.

Strachwitz, Chris and Pete Welding, *American Folk Music Occasional*. New York: Oak Publications, 1970.

Tex-Mex

Dobie, J. Frank, *Texas and Southwestern Lore*. Dallas, TX: Southern Methodist University Press, 1967 [originally published 1927].

Irish

O'Neill, Francis, *Irish Folk Music, A Fascinating Hobby*. Darby, PA: Norwood Reprint, 1973.

Jewish

Sapoznik, Henry, "Jewish Klezmer Music." *In the Tradition* I (1, 2).

Slobin, Mark, ed., *Old Jewish Folk Music*. Philadelphia, PA: University of Pennsylvania Press, 1984.

Norwegian

Blegen, Theodore, and Martin Rand, *Norwegian Emigrant Songs and Ballads*. Minineapolis, MN: Univ. of Minnesota Press, 1937.

 # L·I·S·T·E·N

Cajun Music

Abshire, Nathan. Arhoolie 5013

Abshire, Nathan, *Pine Groove Blues*. Swallow 6014

Abshire, Nathan, *With the Balfa Brothers*. Swallow 6023

Balfa Brothers, *J'Ai Vu Le Loup*. Rounder 6007

Balfa Brothers, *Play Traditional Cajun Music*. Swallow 6011

Balfa, Dewey, *Under the Green Oak Tree*. Arhoolie 5019

Fontenot, Allen, *Jole Blon*. Delta 1118

Hackberry Ramblers. Arhoolie 5003

Louisiana Aces. Rounder 6003

McGee, Dennis. Morningstar 45002

Savoy, Marc, *O What a Night*. Arhoolie 5023

Various, *Cajun Home Music*. Folkways 2620

Various, *Cajun Social Music*. Folkways 2621

Various, *Cajun Songs*. Folkways 4438

Various, *Folksongs of the Louisiana Acadians*. Arhoolie 5009

Various, *J'Etais Au Bal.* Swallow 6020
Various, *Louisiana Cajun Music, Vols. 1–6.* Old Timey 108–111, 114, 124
Various, *Louisiana French Cajun Music, Vols. 1 & 2.* Rounder 6001, 6002
Various, *Music of French America.* Rounder 6010
Various, *The Cajuns.* RBF 21

Zydeco

Chenier, Clifton, *Classic Clifton.* Arhoolie 1082
Chenier, Clifton, *Live.* Arhoolie 1059
Sam Brothers Five, *Lafayette Zydeco.* Arhoolie 1081
Various, *Les Blues de Bayou.* Melodeon 7330
Various, *Louisiana Creole Music* Folkways 2622
Various, *Zodico.* Rounder 6009
Various, *Zydeco.* Arhoolie 1009

Tex-Mex

Conjunto Trio San Antonio. Arhoolie 3004
Jimenez, Flaco, *Y Su Conjunto.* Arhoolie 3007
Jimenez, Santiago and Flaco. Arhoolie 3013
Los Pinguinos del Norte. Arhoolie 3002
Mendoza, Lydia, *La Gloria de Texas.* Arhoolie 3012
Mendoza, Lydia, *Vols. 1 & 2.* Folk Lyric 9023, 9024
Tex-Mex Border Music, *Vol. 1-14.* Folk Lyric 9003-9007, 9011-9013, 9016-20

Irish Immigrants

Burke, Joe, Andy McGann, and Felix Doran, *The Funny Reel.* Shanachie 29012
Byrne, Tom and Tom McCaffrey, *Irish Music in Cleveland, Vols. 1-3.* Folkways
    3517, 3521, 3523
Carroll, Liz, *A Friend Indeed.* Shanachie 29013
Kennedy, Michael J., *65 Years of Irish Music.* June Appal 019
McGann, Andy and Paddy Reynolds. Shanachie 29004
McGreevy, Johnny and Joe Shannon, *The Noonday Feast.* Green Linnet 1023
O'Donnell, Eugene, *Slow Airs & Set Dances.* Green Linnet 1015
Various, *Irish Music on the East Coast.* Rounder 6005
Various, *Irish American Dance Music & Songs.* Folk Lyric 9010
Various, *Irish Traditional Music from Chicago.* Rounder 6006
Various, *Light through the Leaves.* Rounder 6014
Various, *Off to California.* Advent 3601

Jewish Klezmer Music

Feldman, Zev, and Andy Statmen, *Jewish Klezmer Music.* Shanachie 21002
Kapelye, *Future & Past.* Flying Fish 249
Klezmorim, *Metropolis.* Flying Fish 258
Various, *Klezmer Music.* Folkways

Norwegian Music

Nyhus, Sven, *Traditional Norwegian Fiddle Music.* Shanachie 21003

8

Modern country music

From 1920 to today, a revolutionary new music has come out of the Southern and Western United States. Country music is a multi-million dollar industry today, with country stars producing music videos and appearing in large arenas, just like rock 'n' roll performers. However, the country music industry had its birth in the barn dances and community song-swaps of a hundred years ago.

In this chapter, we'll look at the growth of commercial country music, from the original recording stars of the 1920s, through the boom in radio shows, Western swing, the "brother" duets, bluegrass, and finally modern commercial country.

Birth of an Industry

We would know very little about Fiddlin' John Carson, Gid Tanner, Charlie Poole, the Carter Family, or Jimmie Rodgers today if it weren't for two modern inventions: the radio and the phonograph. Without them, these names would be just dim memories. And lesser-known, local artists such as Eck Robertson, Grayson and Whittier, the Hackberry Ramblers, and the Cumberland Ridge Runners (to name just a few) would undoubtedly be forgotten.

Radio was the first medium that helped local artists gain regional (and eventually national) stardom. In the early 1920s, the growth in sales of radios and the emergence of new radio stations nearly destroyed the record industry. Why buy expensive 78 records, that were easily broken and that had to be changed every three minutes, when you could listen to hours of music and entertainment on the radio? This argument convinced one out of three Americans to purchase a radio in the period from 1922 to the stock-market crash of 1929.

Radio stations were established in major cities across the country. The rules for broadcasting were much looser in the 1920s than they are today, so it was not unusual for a radio station operating out of Atlanta to be heard in many other parts of the country, depending on weather conditions and whether another, closer station was operating at a similar frequency. Initially, most radio stations played the same kind of music: popular music that was performed by musicians from New York or Chicago.

However, some enterprising program directors who knew their local audiences, and what they liked to hear, asked local fiddlers and singers to perform their music on the air. The response to the first "barn dance" programs featuring folk musicians was enormous; letters, phone calls, and telegrams flooded stations from listeners anxious to hear more of this "down-home" music. Two pioneers in producing radio shows devoted to traditional music were WLS in Chicago and WSM in Nashville. WSM's show, originally broadcast in 1925, became known as "The Grand Ole Opry," and it has become the most influential showcase for country performers in the world.

Prior to the early 1920s, the record industry did little to record traditional musicians. Occasionally, a fiddle record was issued as a novelty item, but no effort was made to market country music to country folk. However, the success of radio led to a decline in record sales. Executives were frantic to discover new markets. Meanwhile, local record dealers realized the potential for country performers.

In Atlanta, the local furniture dealer—who also sold phonographs and records—recommended a fiddling ballad singer, known as Fiddlin' John Carson (1868–1949), to New York-based OKeh records. The recording executive who made the first record, "Little Old Log Cabin in the Lane" (a sentimental song telling the story of an old countryman, his dog, and his ramshackle home), and "The Old Hen Cackled and the Rooster's Going to Crow" (a fiddle tune imitating the sounds of chickens in the barnyard), thought that it was so bad that he had it specially issued, without a label or a catalogue number, for sale only in Atlanta. The unlabelled record sold out almost immediately, and the country-music record industry was born.

The First Stars

The Pioneers: Carson, Tanner, Poole, and Macon

Fiddlin' John Carson, the singer/fiddler who made such a hit with "The Little Old Log Cabin in the Lane," was in his 50s when he was first recorded. He was well-known in Georgia as a local star of country fairs and dances, bringing a good-humored approach to singing, and playing primarily recently composed sentimental songs and the traditional dance tunes of the mountains. He often appeared with his daughter, who he called "Moonshine Kate"; she played the guitar and served as a deadpan foil to her father's humorous showmanship.

Carson was typical of many generations of amateur performers who worked as laborers in factories or fields in order to support themselves, and augmented these earnings by performing music for dances in homes, town halls, and country fairs. The most talented of this pool of musicians could occasionally find employment with a traveling tent show. These shows were organized by manufacturers of popular "home remedies" (patent medicines). When the tent show arrived in a small town, it was sure to attract attention; every performance opened and closed with a special pitch for the latest medicine. Although medicine shows were organized to make money for the drug companies, they also helped spread the music of people like John Carson through a much larger area than otherwise would have been possible.

The success of John Carson's first records led other companies to seek out similar fiddler/singers. Columbia records discovered in Georgia James Gideon (Gid) Tanner (1885–1960), who was from the same generation as Carson and performed in a similar style. Tanner was often accompanied by a blind singer/guitarist, George Riley Puckett (1890–1946). Puckett was one of the first guitarists to move beyond simply playing chords to accompany dance tunes to experimenting with using "bass runs," special patterns played on the lower strings of the guitar. He also sang in a smooth, almost crooning style, and would become a very popular performer of country songs in the years ahead, sort of a country Bing Crosby.

Record executives at Columbia were anxious to exploit the talents of Tanner and Puckett in a larger band setting. They found the perfect match of talents in another Georgia-based group, the "Lick the Skillet" band, featuring a young, jazz-influenced fiddler named Clayton (Mac) McMichen (1900–1970). The new group was christened "Gid Tanner and his Skillet Lickers," and from 1926 to 1931 they were one of the most influential and successful string bands in the country.

The Skillet Lickers featured two, three, or four fiddles taking the lead, giving them a powerful, driving melody section. McMichen excelled at playing high-energy dance music, keeping perfect time with clean intonation (definition of each note). He assembled a top-notch fiddle section capable of playing in perfect unison and of producing modern harmonies. Tanner, a more old-fashioned musician, often did not play fiddle at all on these records; instead, he contributed falsetto vocals (singing at the top of his vocal range), and comic effects. Puckett's guitar playing emphasized the tight rhythms produced by the fiddlers. Although a banjo player was a member of the band, his part can hardly be heard on the recordings.

Other string bands rose to meet the challenge of the Skillet Lickers. Charlie Poole and his North Carolina Ramblers were one of the most popular. Like the Skillet Lickers, they performed a combination of dance music and sentimental songs. However, they played in a style that was totally different than the Georgia band. The Ramblers were a three-piece band, made up of fiddle, banjo, and guitar. The fiddle playing was less rhythmic than the raucous Skillet Lickers' style; the fiddler emphasized the notes of the melody, rather than its rhythm. The guitar playing was more subdued than Puckett's work. But most unusual was the banjo playing of Charlie Poole (1892–1931), the group's leader.

Poole was a country-born banjo player who was influenced by early 20th-century recordings by city-based banjoists like Fred Van Epps. These city banjo players picked the banjo with their fingers; country banjo players had traditionally played in the frailing or clawhammer style (see Chapter 5). Poole played in this city-influenced picking style, producing rolling chords on his banjo that sound something like the bluegrass banjo styles that are popular today.

The Bogtrotters from Galax, VA. Featuring Wade Ward (banjo), Fields Ward (guitar), and Crockett Ward (seated fiddler). PHOTOGRAPH: Alan Lomax. Reproduction from the Collections of the Library of Congress.

Another important figure in the history of country music is Uncle Dave Macon (1870–1952), a banjo player and entertainer from Tennessee. Like Carson and Tanner, he represented an older generation of musician who had travelled with tent shows and performed for local parties. Macon was quite a showman, introducing each piece with a comical monologue and ending every performance with a brash, vivacious laugh. He played the banjo in both frailing and picking styles, and like Carson and Tanner performed a mix of folk songs, dance tunes, and more recently composed songs. He was a popular performer on the Grand Ole Opry through the 1940s, remaining a powerful reminder of country music's heritage.

Smooth Singers: Jimmie Rodgers and the Carter Family

Jimmie Rodgers (1897–1933) is often credited with being the first country performer to reach a national audience. He had worked on the railroads in Mississippi, gaining the name of "The Singing Brakeman." Rodgers played the guitar in a very simple style; the emphasis was on his smooth vocals and his characteristic Swiss yodel. He even made some records with band accompaniments (jazz-trumpeter Louis Armstrong appeared on one recording!). Rodgers life ended tragically when he died of tuberculosis; however, his death stimulated a cult that had been growing among his fans, and his records continue to sell well today.

Rodgers is important for another reason: many of his songs were in the form of "blues" numbers, like "T.B. Blues" and "T for Texas." Although his style of singing was smooth, his choice of material was influenced by Black traditions. Rodgers paved the way for the acceptance of Black singers among White audiences by popularizing Black song styles.

The Carter Family were friends of Jimmie Rodgers, and were also smooth, modern performers of traditional folk music. A. (Alvin) P. (Pleasant) Carter (1891-1960) was the head of the family, hailing originally from rural Virginia; he had a knack for finding traditional songs that could be arranged in more modern settings. His wife Sara (1899-1979), sang lead with the group and played autoharp; his sister-in-law, Maybelle Addington Carter (1909-1978), sang alto and played guitar, autoharp, and banjo; A.P. sang the bass part. The trio recorded hundreds of songs from the 1920s to the 1940s; as children were born, they were added to the travelling revue. One of the Carter children, June Carter (1929-   ), has gone on to a successful singing career as the wife and musical partner of Johnny Cash (1932-   ); their daughter Roseanne Cash (1955-   ) continues the family business of making music.

The Carter family emphasized vocals over accompaniment. They were one of the first folk groups that did not play any dance music. This shift away from rollicking fiddles to harmonized voices had a huge impact on the growth of country music from its folk roots into a major commercial industry.

Western Swing

Out in the Southwest, the influence of radio and the phonograph was changing the face of dance-band music. Fiddlers were hooking up with rhythm players (guitar-bass-drums) who were skilled in modern jazz styles; soon the bands grew to include jazz and pop instruments, including trumpets, tenor banjos, honky tonk piano, and even the accordion. One of the pioneers in this field was Texas-born fiddler Bob Wills (1905-1975).

Wills's early life story is remarkably similar to Gid Tanner, Fiddlin' John Carson, and hundreds of other folk fiddlers. He learned to play at his father's knee. At the age of 19, he joined a travelling show, where he augmented his fiddle playing by performing in black face in comic skits. Wills soon hooked up with a guitarist and a vocalist, and the three left the show to perform in small bars and dance joints.

Desperate for extra income, the trio approached a large company to be their sponsor; the Burrus Flour Mills produced "Light Crust" bread, a popular item in all Southern homes. The company saw in the trio a chance to promote their products. The band members worked in the mills by day, and promoted the mills' product by performing on weekend nights. The new group was christened the Light Crust Doughboys.

Wills left the band soon thereafter and formed his own Texas Playboys. This became the model for most Western swing bands that followed. The band featured two or three fiddles, playing in harmony, taking the melody lead. A rollicking pianist, playing in a style influenced by ragtime, jazz, and boogie-woogie, was usually featured. The strong rhythm section consisted of tenor banjo, bass, and drums that kept a loud, regular beat.

Wills also featured a new instrument, the electric lap or slide guitar, known as the "lap steel." This is an electric guitar that is held in the lap; the player tunes the instrument so that the strings, when unfretted, produce a chord. (This type of tuning is called "open tuning," because the unfretted or open strings play a chord.) In the left or fretting hand, the player uses a metal bar to slide up and down the strings, in order to produce gliding chords and melody notes. The first great player of the lap steel was Leon McAuliffe

(1917-   ), a member of Wills's band. In later years, the lap steel was enlarged, with more strings and necks added, until eventually it grew into today's pedal steel guitar.

For many years, the Texas Playboys featured Tommy Duncan on lead vocals. Duncan hardly sounds like a country singer at all. In fact, his style is clearly influenced by Bing Crosby and other jazz-age crooners. While Duncan sang in the smooth style, Wills often added his own two cents, yodelling, talking, or singing along in his high-pitched, distinctive country voice. It's almost as if the country audience was responding to the city-slicker's music by adding its own humorous commentary.

Western Swing was most popular in the middle 1930s through the 1940s. Today, the Western Swing sound has been incorporated into mainstream country bands.

Brother Acts and Bluegrass

In the 1930s, several folk duos performed who specialized in singing in tight harmonies. A number of these acts were made up of paired siblings, and so have become known as the "brother acts." The Delmore Brothers, the Blue Sky Boys (the Bolick brothers), and the Monroe Brothers were three of the most successful acts in this style.

All three acts featured smooth, harmonized vocals. In each case, one brother sang lead, while the other provided a high tenor harmony part, influenced by the mountain style of singing in an intense, breathy tone (Chapter 5). Most of the songs that they performed were either new compositions about life in the mountains and the changing life in the rural South, or the sentimental songs of the late 19th century.

Alton (1908-1964) and Rabon (1910-1952) Delmore hailed from Alabama, and their guitar work shows the influence of Black blues performers in the syncopated lead parts. Both brothers played guitars, one playing a six-string, the other a four-string or tenor guitar. Although the guitar accompaniments to the vocals were subdued, they often took jazzy solos between the verses. Their repertory was largely based on folk blues, including their big hit "Brown's Ferry Blues."

The Blue Sky Boys were the most traditional in approach. Bill Bolick (1917-   ) sang the high tenor and played the mandolin; his brother Earl (1919-   ) took the baritone part and played the guitar. Their repertory was drawn from traditional songs and more recently composed ones, and they favored songs that dealt with tragic love, natural disasters, or sorrowful events. Many of their harmony parts were quite complex, featuring call and response between the two voices or interweaving harmony lines. In a sense, neither voice sang the lead part; both parts were combined to form a single lead. The Bolicks featured instrumental breaks, just as did the Delmores, although the mandolin playing of Bill Bolick was fairly simple.

The Monroe Brothers were most influential in introducing hot, jazz-influenced mandolin playing to country music in the middle '30s. Bill Monroe (1911-   ) is one of country music's legendary performers. He possesses a crystal-clear, high tenor voice that is instantly recognizable. The mandolin solos that he recorded with his brother were dazzling, featuring many quick runs and fiery parts that had an intensity never before heard in country music. Bill's brother Charlie (1903-1975) provided the lead vocals and guitar accompaniments that were the underpinnings for Bill's virtuosity.

The Birth of Bluegrass

In 1938, Bill Monroe left his brother and struck out on his own. He found the guitar-mandolin format too limited for his considerable talents. Monroe's music had been formed by a boyhood in Kentucky listening to the country fiddling of his Uncle Pen Vanderver; he was also exposed at an early age to Black traditions through several local blues guitarists. Western swing music was sweeping the country, and Monroe longed to find a format for his own music that was as exciting as this Texas style. It wasn't until 1945 when Monroe met banjo player Earl Scruggs (1924-   ) and singer/guitarist Lester Flatt (1914-1979) that he was able to form his first truly great band.

Scruggs was a banjo player from North Carolina who learned to play in the finger-picking style of Charlie Poole and other Carolinians. During his boyhood, he was influenced by a distant relative who picked with three fingers, rather than the ordinary two. By adding the extra picking finger, Scruggs was able to play melodies and rolls (several notes, making up a chord, played in rapid succession) in a loud, driving style that transformed the banjo from an accompaniment to a lead instrument. Scruggs's style is the model for all bluegrass players who followed.

Flatt was a vocalist whose smooth delivery perfectly complemented the intensity of Monroe's harmonies. Flatt's vocals incorporated the easy, relaxed style of a pop singer, with the ornamented intensity of mountain singing.

Bill Monroe's band, called the Blue Grass Boys (after the Kentucky state motto, "the bluegrass state"), is considered the classic bluegrass band. Today, most bands feature the same five-man, instrumental lineup: guitar-fiddle-mandolin-banjo-bass. Monroe's

Cowhands singing after a day's work, Quarter Circle "U" Ranch roundup, Big Horn County, Montana. PHOTOGRAPH: Arthur Rothstein, 1940. Reproduction from the Collections of the Library of Congress.

compositions, songs like "Blue Moon of Kentucky" and "Uncle Pen" and instrumentals like "Raw Hide" and "Scotland," have become bluegrass classics.

Other bands have followed in Monroe's footsteps. Flatt and Scruggs left the master's band in the late 1940s to form their own group, performing together for nearly 20 years. They became international stars when their music was featured in the film "Bonnie and Clyde." Ralph (1927-   ) and Carter (1925-1966) Stanley, two brothers from Southern Virginia, formed a traditional bluegrass band in the late 1940s, following the Monroe mold. Ralph's high-intensity harmonies and simple bluegrass banjo picking, and Carter's abilities as songwriter and lead singer, quickly made them famous. Today, following Carter's death, Ralph continues to play traditional bluegrass with a strong element of mountain singing in it.

Country Music Comes to the City

The folk music revival of the 1940s and 1950s (see Chapter 9) led to a new interest in country music. One of the first groups to revive the country string-band style was the New Lost City Ramblers, founded in the late 1950s by Mike Seeger (1933-   ), John Cohen (1932-   ), and Tom Paley (1928-   ). These city-bred musicians were also folklorists, travelling to out-of-the-way communities to rediscover and record the country stars of the 1920s and 30s. The Ramblers influenced an entire generation of fiddlers, banjo players, and guitarists, through both their music and their scholarship.

Bluegrass music suffered a dip in popularity in the 1950s when rock 'n' roll burst on the scene. In the 1960s, the folk revival gave a new audience for bluegrass performers on college campuses and at folk festivals. Meanwhile, new city groups were formed, including the Greenbriar Boys and the Country Gentlemen. Bluegrass players in the city began to experiment with new ways of using the basic instruments and also began incorporating rhythms and riffs from blues, rock, and jazz. This led in the 1970s to "newgrass," a wedding of bluegrass traditions with new influences, performed by such groups as the New Grass Revival and Country Cooking.

In Nashville, the capital of commercial country music, the smooth vocalists, singing in a style derived from mainstream pop music, were dominating the airways and recording dates. Singer Roy Acuff (1903-   ), coming from a mountain background, began his career as a fiddler in the 1930s, but soon switched to singing and writing country classics. In the 1950s, honky-tonk country music predominated; singers often performed with heavy rhythm accompaniments of guitar-fiddle-steel guitar-drums. The greatest in this genre was Hank Williams (1923-1953), who carried on the tradition of Jimmie Rodgers in his vocal style, including many yodels and leaps into the upper octaves of his voice. Williams' recording of "Lovesick Blues," originally a jazz tune, propelled him to stardom in 1949, and his premature death in 1953 has assured him a place as one of country music's legends.

Women have always played an important role in country music. Rose Maddox (1926-   ) performed along with her brothers through the 1940s and 1950s in a Western-Swing style band. Maddox popularized a powerful style of singing, perhaps to overpower the noise and inattentiveness of the typical honky-tonk audience. Patsy Cline (1932-1963) was a major star in the late 1950s. Her style is more refined than Maddox's, although it too shows clear mountain heritage. Loretta Lynn (1935-   ) came on the scene in the mid-1960s, and is today's most popular, traditionally based singer. Although her repertoire is made up of recently composed material, her voice is pure country; she will ornament a melody using trills, slides, and grace notes just as a ballad singer from the mountains might do. Her strong, straight-ahead delivery is part of the mountain style.

In the 1960s, country music seemed to lose some of its direction, with musical arrangements that featured heavy use of string sections, and songs that reflected a conservative backlash against the Civil Rights/peace movement of the era. Beginning in the 1970s, country singers began to court wider audiences by incorporating elements of rock arrangements in their records. Today, country music stars range from the traditionalists, like Ricky Scaggs (1954-   ), who have revived acoustic instruments and older songs, to flashy good-time groups, like Alabama, who are similar in performance style and instrumentation to any other Top-40 rock band.

R·E·A·D

Artis, Bob, *Bluegrass*. Hawthorn Books, 1975

Carawan, Guy and Candie, *Voices from the Mountains*. New York: Knopf, 1975.

Cohen, John, and Mike Seeger, *Old Time Stringband Songbook*. New York: Oak Publications, 1976.

Green, Archie, *Only a Miner*. Champaign, IL: University of Illinois Press, 1972.

Green, Douglas B., *Country Roots: The Origins of Country Music*. New York: Hawthorne, 1976.

Guralnick, Peter, *Lost Highway*. Boston, MA: David Godine, 1979.

Horstman, Dorothy, *Sing Your Heart Out, Country Boy*. Nashville, TN: Country Music Foundation Press, 1986.

Hurst, Jack, *Grand Ole Opry*. New York: Abrams, 1975.

Lynn, Loretta, with George Vecsey, *Loretta Lynn: Coal Miner's Daughter*. New York: Warner, 1976.

Malone, Bill, *Country Music USA* (2nd Revised Edition). Austin, TX: University of Texas Press, 1985.

Malone, Bill C., *Southern Music, American Music*. Lexington, KY: Univ. of Kentucky Press, 1979.

Oermann, Robert K., with Douglas B. Green, *The Listener's Guide to Country Music*. New York: Facts on File, 1983.

Porterfield, Nolan, *Jimmie Rodgers: The Life and Times of America's Blue Yodeler*. Champaign, IL: Univ. of Illinois Press, 1979.

Rooney, James, *Bossmen: Bill Monroe and Muddy Waters*. New York: Dial Press, 1971.

Shelton, Robert and Burt Goldblatt, *The Country Music Story*. New York: Castle, 1966.

Townsend, Charles R., *San Antonio Rose: The Life and Music of Bob Wills*. Champaign, IL: Univ. of Illinois Press, 1976.

Wolfe, Charles K., *The Grand Ole Opry: The Early Years*. London: Old Time Music, 1975.

L·I·S·T·E·N

Early Stars of Country Music

Blue Sky Boys. Rounder 0052
Blue Sky Boys, *Sunny Side of Life*. Rounder 1006
Carson, Fiddlin' John, *Old Hen Cackled . . .* Rounder 1003
Carter Family, *In Texas, Vols. 1-5*. Old Homestead 111, 112, 116, 117, 130
Carter Family, *On Border Radio*. JEMF 101
Delmore Brothers, *Brown's Ferry Blues*. County 402
Macon, Uncle Dave. County 521
Macon, Uncle Dave. RBF 51
Macon, Uncle Dave, *Go 'Long Mule*. County 545
Monroe Brothers, *Feast Here Tonight*. Bluebird AXM-2-5510
Monroe, Charlie, *Early Years*. Old Homestead 133
Monroe, Charlie, *Noonday Jamboree*. County 538
Poole, Charlie, *Vol. 1, 2, 3, 4*. County 505, 508, 516, 540
Puckett, Riley, *Waiting for the Evening Mail*. County 411
The Skillet Lickers, *Hear These New . . . Records*. Rounder 1005
Various, *Country Music: South and West*. New World 287
Various, *Going Down the Valley*. New World 236
Various, *Hell Broke Loose in Georgia*. County 514
Various, *Kentucky Fiddle Band Music, Vols. 1-3*. Morningstar 45003-45005
Various, *Mr. Charlie's Blues*. Yazoo 1024
Various, *Nashville: The Early String Bands*. County 541, 542
Various, *String Band, Vols. 1 & 2*. Old Timey 100, 101
Various, *Western Swing, Vols. 1-8*. Old Timey 105, 116, 117, 119-123

Bluegrass

Baker, Kenny, *Bluegrass Fiddler*. County 719
Baker, Kenny, *Plays Bill Monroe*. County 761
Country Gazette, *American & Clean*. Flying Fish 253
Flatt, Lester and Earl Scruggs, *Golden Era*. Rounder SS05
Flatt, Lester and Earl Scruggs, *Golden Years*. County 101
Flatt, Lester and the Nashville Grass, Greatest Performances. CMH 6238
Hot Rize. Flying Fish 206
McReynolds, Jim and Jesse, *Story*. CMH 9022
Monroe, Bill, *Original Bluegrass Band*. Rounder SS06
Monroe, Bill and his Bluegrass Boys, *Classic Bluegrass Recordings, Vols. 1 & 2*.
    County 104, 105
Sparks, Larry, *John Deere Tractor*. Rebel 1588
Stanley Brothers, *The Best*. Starday/King 953
Stanley, Brothers, *Vols. 1 & 2*. Rounder SS09, 10
Stanley, Ralph, *Old Country Church*. Rebel 1508
Stanley, Ralph, *On and On*. County 776
Various, *Early Days, Vols. 1-10*. Rounder 1013-1022
Various, *Mountain Music Bluegrass Style*. Folkways 2318
Various, *Thirty Years of Bluegrass*. New World 225

9

The folk music revival

The Seeds of the Revival

The folk music revival really began about 200 years ago. At that time, a new mood was sweeping Europe, leading to revolutionary changes in governments and the way people lived. Working-class people were gaining power, while the aristocracy (or upper classes) was losing it. In America, a revolution led to the ousting of British rule and the establishment of a new democracy. With a new emphasis on the importance of the people came a new interest in the arts of the people, including folk music and dance. Scholars in England and America published collections of this music to celebrate the achievements of the ordinary folk.

In the United States, the folk music revival began with the publication of important collections of songs. John Avery Lomax (1875-1948) was one of the best-known American folksong scholars. Self-trained in the study of folksong, Lomax collected hundreds of examples of ballads and songs from cowboys in the mid-West. His book, *Cowboy Songs and Other Frontier Ballads*, appeared in 1910 with an introduction by Teddy Roosevelt, who praised Lomax for preserving "the unwritten ballad literature of the back country and the frontier."

By 1910, the frontier in America was already disappearing. Cities were growing, and farmers and cowhands were leaving the land to work in factories and mills. Lomax's *Cowboy Songs* hit a sensitive nerve, appealing to people's nostalgia for a simpler time, when

John A. Lomax shaking hands with "Uncle" Rick Brown. 1940. Reproduction from the Collections of the Library of Congress.

men could still make a living by working the land. As the life of the backwoodsman disappeared, folklorists rushed to record their music, dances, and stories. Lomax was important in inspiring many others to travel through the country and collect America's musical heritage.

In the 1930s, John Lomax was joined by his son Alan (1915–) in a trip to Mississippi to collect songs from Black prisoners. During this trip, they met an inmate with unusual talents; he was a skilled musician (playing the 12-string guitar), sang in a powerful tenor voice, and composed his own songs. He was recognized by prisoners and jailers alike as one of the greatest performer in the region. His name was Huddie Ledbetter (1885-1949); his size and power earned him the nickname Leadbelly. The Lomaxes returned to the Northern cities with enough material to fill a book on Leadbelly; soon Leadbelly would follow them. He was one of the first traditional folk musicians to perform for a city audience.

Pete Seeger, Woody Guthrie, and the Weavers

Leadbelly soon befriended a young, scrawny banjo player, the son of a famous musicologist, who was working as an assistant to Alan

Lomax. The banjo player had just begun performing for small meetings of union members, in churches, at fairs, and for groups of his radical friends. His name was Pete Seeger (1919-   ).

Seeger came from a musical family, but also a family with strong ties to business and tradition. Following in the family folksteps, Seeger began what was to be training for a business career at Harvard, but soon dropped out of school, long before dropping out was fashionable. Instead of studying books, he longed to study people. With his banjo, he travelled South in search of traditional musicians.

Folk music appealed to Seeger for two reasons: he loved the vitality of Southern banjo music, the energetic dance tunes and songs that he learned from the banjo players that he met. He also loved folk music because it represented the real music of the people. Seeger was deeply involved with groups who were struggling to help ordinary people. In the 1930s, during the depths of the Great Depression, many people were out of work, some lost their homes, while others could barely afford to put food on the table. Wages were low, and working conditions were poor. Unions were organized to help workers; Seeger lent his banjo and song to union meetings to inspire others to enroll in the fight against poverty.

During his trips across the country, Seeger performed at many concerts and rallies to benefit different causes. In early 1940, he appeared in California at a concert to benefit migrant farm workers; here he met a wiry, intense singer, guitarist, and songwriter who originally hailed from Okemah, Oklahoma. His name was Wood-row Wilson (Woody) Guthrie (1912-1967).

Guthrie was everything Seeger was not. Seeger came from a prosperous, middle-class Eastern family; Guthrie came from a dirt-poor family from the West. Seeger's parents were educated and talented musicians; Guthrie's father was a failure as a farmer and his mother was confined to an asylum, suffering from Huntington's chorea, a degenerative nerve disease. Pete had never seen the country; Woody had been a hobo for years. Seeger had just begun his career as a performer, and was nervous on stage; Guthrie had played on the radio in California, and had performed for groups large and small all throughout the West. Soon, he would record his famous "Dust Bowl Ballads," which immortalized the plight of the small farmers who lost their land in the terrible Oklahoma dust storms of the 1930s.

Guthrie's contribution to American folk music was enormous, despite the fact that he was not an outstanding guitarist or singer; in fact, his playing was just adequate. However, he sang with great depth of feeling, and his voice, although rough and untrained, was perfectly suited to his songs about life in America's small farms, factories, and urban centers. His songs remain classics to this day, and there is hardly anyone in this country who doesn't know "This Land is Your Land" or "So Long, It's Been Good to Know You," two Guthrie classics.

When Seeger and Guthrie returned to New York, they were joined by a group of singers, musicians, and actors in an informal group called the Almanac Singers. The Almanacs performed for meetings and rallies, usually for a special cause. The group didn't have a fixed membership; it changed on different evenings when different people were available to play.

World War II brought a temporary halt to the singing and songwriting on the streets of New York. After the war, Guthrie began to feel the effects of the disease that he inherited from his mother, Huntington's chorea. He was soon confined to a hospital, unable to play. Seeger joined with a new group of singers who had been associated with Peoples' Songs. Fred Hellerman (1927-   ), Lee Hays (1914-1984), Ronnie Gilbert, and Seeger formed the Weavers, for the purpose of popularizing folk song with a larger audience. They soon had a record contract with Decca records, and a number-one hit with "Goodnight Irene."

The Weavers were an important group for a number of reasons. Although they sang in a more polished style than traditional singers, they still sounded very unusual when compared with Bing Crosby or Frank Sinatra, two smooth-voiced crooners who enjoyed great popularity in the '40s. The Weavers drew on a repertory of songs not only from the United States, but from far-off places like Israel and South Africa. Their sole accompaniment was Hellerman's guitar and Seeger's banjo, which both played very understated roles. There were no heavy strings, no brass sections, or any drums on their records. And, when the Weavers performed, they encouraged the audience to sing along, something that was unheard of at that time.

The Weavers' career was cut short when they were branded as "communists" by the House Committee on Un-American Activities. Seeger and his bandmates had played for union rallies, marched in parades against unfair working conditions, and they had even performed and worked for the American Communist Party, which in the 1930s was working to improve conditions for the underpriviledged. In the 1950s, these activities were considered crimes; soon Seeger was unable to find work anywhere.

The 1960's Folk Boom

The seeds that the Weavers had planted would blossom some 10 years later in a boom in folk music. The folk musicians of the

The Weavers in a Reunion photo taken in the early 1960s. L to r: Erik Darling, unknown, Ronnie Gilbert, Fred Hellerman, Lee Hays, Peter Seeger, Frank Hamilton. PHOTO COURTESY: Vanguard Records.

1960s took their inspiration from Seeger and Guthrie to perform a wide variety of musical styles. Some followed directly in the footsteps of the Weavers, forming commercial groups that scored Top-10 hits with their popular arrangements of traditional songs. Others carefully sought to recreate Southern string-band music or rural blues. Still others took folk music as a springboard to create their own music.

Popular Folk Groups

In the early 1960s, the Kingston Trio scored a Top-10 hit with "Tom Dooley," an old Southern banjo song that told the story of a ne'er-do-well who was going to die on the gallows. The Kingston Trio, like the Weavers, performed with simple guitar/banjo accompaniment. They sang in a smooth, polished style, performed in neat jackets like you might see fraternity brothers wearing, and were very popular in nightclubs and on college campuses. The success of the Kingston Trio inspired countless imitations: the Wayfarers, even a revived form of the Weavers, with Erik Darling (1933-   ) taking the place of Pete Seeger.

One group that stood apart from the rest was Peter, Paul, and

Mary. Peter Yarrow (1938-   ), Noel Paul Stookey (1937-   ) and Mary Travers (1937-   ) were regulars at many Greenwich Village, New York clubs. Like many others, they had listened to the Weavers' records, and were familiar with the songs of Woody Guthrie and Leadbelly. They began singing together, with Mary's powerful and polished vocals taking the lead, and the two men providing harmony and guitar parts. One of their first hits was a song that was coauthored by Seeger and Lee Hays, "If I Had a Hammer." Peter, Paul, and Mary's recording of this song became the battle cry and inspiration for many '60s gatherings to fight for civil rights for America's Blacks and to protest against America's involvement in the Vietnam War.

Bob Dylan and the Protest Singers

Peter, Paul, and Mary introduced another protest song that was to have a lasting impact on America; it was called "Blowin' in the Wind," and its author was a young singer/guitarist from Minnesota, Robert Allen Zimmerman (1941-   ), known today as Bob Dylan.

Dylan came to New York to meet Woody Guthrie. He had heard Guthrie's records, and idolized his singing style and method of writing topical songs to folk melodies. Dylan walked, talked, lived, and breathed the life of Woody Guthrie. Like Guthrie, Dylan was not a talented guitarist nor was he a great singer. But like his idol, he had a knack for putting his personal thoughts into songs that would serve as anthems for his generation.

Prior to the success of Bob Dylan, it was quite unusual for a popular star to also be a songwriter. In the old days, songwriters weren't expected to perform their material. Songwriters were professionals, and it was understood that the words that they wrote didn't actually reflect their experiences. Dylan added personal emotions to his songs, and he expanded the vocabulary of the popular songwriter to include references to French poets, Indian religions, the Bible, and esoteric folk figures, all culled from his personal interests or experiences. Dylan, by following the model of Woody Guthrie, changed the way popular music is made. Now, anyone could buy a guitar, learn a few chords, and express their feelings through song.

Dylan's early songs generally address social issues, and so have been called "protest" or "topical" songs. "Blowin' in the Wind" was inspired by the Civil Rights movement, and many White Americans' resistance to accept Blacks on equal terms; "A Hard Rain's A-Gonna Fall" addresses the problem of nuclear fallout. Dylan was joined in the protest movement by several other talented performers and songwriters. Joan Baez (1941-   ) helped launch topical songs to a larger audience; her highly trained voice and youthful good looks made her much in demand throughout the 1960s. She was one of the first singers to use her popularity to address current issues, such as civil rights and the Vietnam War.

Phil Ochs (1940-1976) was a more satiric songwriter and performer than Dylan, who enjoyed great success in the mid-1960s. Many of his songs made strong comments about current events, including the Bay of Pigs fiasco ("The Cuban Invasion"), the Vietnam War ("I Ain't Marching Anymore"), and the resistance to civil rights in the South ("Here's to the State of Mississippi").

Other social protest singers include Tom Paxton (1937-   ), who wrote many folk standards including "Bottle of Wine" and the ever-popular "Ramblin' Boy," and Buffy Sainte-Marie (1941-   ), who scored a big hit with "The Universal Soldier," an antiwar classic, and wrote many songs reflecting her American Indian heritage.

The Stringband and Blues Revivals

Pete Seeger had an enormous impact on the first generation of folk revivalists; he continued to perform through the 1960s and 1970s, but now represented an older generation. His younger half-brother Mike (1933-   ) was to be an important figure to the next generation of folk performers.

Pete Seeger interprets folk music; he has evolved a banjo style that is uniquely his own, even though it is based on traditional folk styles. He is not afraid to change the words to songs, or the melodies, or the chords. Mike Seeger began his career trying to recreate exactly how folk music was performed a half a century ago. He was careful not to change a thing, not to try to commercialize the music or to make it easier for modern listeners to enjoy it.

Mike Seeger joined with two other musicians, banjo-player John Cohen (1932-   ) and guitarist Tom Paley (1928-   ), to form a string band called the New Lost City Ramblers. The Ramblers were the first and most influential groups to abandon the polished style of the Weavers or the Kingston Trio to try to authentically recreate the music of the Southern mountains. They influenced countless others to learn to play in traditional mountain fiddle, banjo, and guitar styles.

In the 1970s, the Ramblers were joined by younger bands who took a more creative approach to folk traditions, using the folk styles of the Southern mountains as the basis for writing new tunes and rearranging old ones. Some of these bands included the popular Highwoods Stringband, that took a wild, high-energy approach to dance music, and the more subdued Fuzzy Mountain Stringband. One group, the Red Clay Ramblers, has broadened the string band style to include blues, jazz, early rock, and their own compositions.

Mike Seeger was important to the folk music revival not merely as a performer but also as a folklorist. He made many trips to the South to search out many of the performers who had recorded in the 1920s and '30s. Through his efforts, important musicians such as Dock Boggs (1898-1971), a bluesy-sounding banjo player, and Elizabeth Cotten, a finger-style guitarist and songwriter from North Carolina, were recorded and introduced to concert stages throughout the world.

Another group of folklorists and performers focussed their attention on the music of Black blues guitarists. They were particularly interested in the rural blues recorded in the 1920s and '30s. Dave van Ronk (1936-   ), a White guitarist popular in New York City, led the blues revival by faithfully recreating the guitar and vocal styles of the blues masters. Other performers, like Tom Rush (1941-   ), began by emulating blues singers, but soon moved on to performing their own compositions.

Folk Rock

Many of the folk performers of the early 1960s moved on to play rock and popular music in the later years of that decade. It was a natural progression from working as popular performers to pick up electric instruments and try to appeal to a larger audience.

For many, the switch to electric guitars, bass, and drums was a result of the success of the Beatles. The Beatles spearheaded what was called the "British Invasion" of American popular music. Actually, the Beatles were themselves inspired by American rock and roll artists of the '50s, so that they were in a sense reintroducing America to its own music. But, it was mostly the Beatles sound, an upbeat combination of sweet vocal harmonies and bright electric guitars, that inspired American performers.

Two performers who had been playing in popular folk bands were Jim McGuinn* and David Crosby. Both were talented musicians who had performed as soloists in small coffeehouses and as backup musicians for other performers. Both were impressed with the sound of the Beatles. McGuinn was a fan of the songwriting of Bob Dylan, which had only reached a folk audience in the early 1960s. With three other musicians, McGuinn and Crosby formed the Byrds; their first release was an electrified version of Dylan's "Mr. Tambourine Man." The record was a runaway best-seller. The Byrds combined soft, folky harmonies with the distinctive sound of McGuinn's electrified 12-string guitar, setting the pattern for many folk rock groups to come.

*McGuinn changed his name to Roger in the late 1960s.

In England, a group of musicians centering around Ashley Hutch-
ings was also intrigued with the music of Dylan and other young
songwriters. They banded together to form Fairport Convention.
The group reached its peak when it recorded an album made up
of traditional English ballads, with an accompaniment of electric
guitars, electrified fiddle, bass, and drums. This album, titled *Liege
and Lief*, proved that folk music could be as "contemporary" as the
latest songs.

Folk rock performers have earned a permanent place in American
music. Some are singer/songwriters, following in the footsteps of
Woody Guthrie and Bob Dylan. Arlo Guthrie (1947-   ),
Woody's son, was influenced as much by Bob Dylan as he was by
his famous parent; he achieved his first hit with a comical "talking
blues" number, "Alice's Restaurant." John Denver gained fame in
the 1970s as the spokesman for environmental concerns in his
songs "Country Roads" and "Rocky Mountain High." James Taylor
also comes out of the singer/songwriter tradition, but expresses
mostly personal concerns. The Eagles are perhaps the best-known
of all folk-rock groups. Their music spans everything from
mainstream rock to country ballads.

Folk Record Producers

The boom in folk music could hardly have occurred if it weren't
for a few visionary producers of records and books. By the mid-
1960s, it wasn't necessary to visit a special archive or library to
hear the blues from the Mississippi Delta, the country banjo sounds
of North Carolina, or the accordion music of the Mexican immigrants of Texas. You could simply visit a well-stocked folk music
record shop.

The granddaddy of all folk record labels is Folkways Records of
New York. Founder Moses Asch (1905-1986) was the son of
novelist Sholem Asch, and an early pioneer of recording
techniques. He established Folkways in the late 1940s in order to
document "everything occurring on the earth and in the contemporary time," in his own words. Today, the Folkways catalog is a
living monument to the vision of its founder, with records on
diverse subjects from the sounds of a rain forest, to the words of a
modern poet, to the banjo styles of Pete Seeger, to the music from
the Aborigines of Australia. Folkways has close to 2,000 albums
in its catalog, issued from 1947 to today, all still in print.

Many small labels have followed in Folkways' footsteps. Some
are broad-based labels that feature a wide variety of musics; others

specialize in a single area. Arhoolie Records of California specializes in blues, Tex-Mex, and contemporary folk. Rounder Records, founded as a collective in the early 1970s, began its life as a bluegrass and old-time music label, but has expanded to include British traditions, singer/songwriters, mainstream country, and blues. Yazoo Records, founded by Nick Perls in New York City, specializes in reissuing 78 recordings of blues and early jazz. Flying Fish of Chicago is the most commercially oriented of the folk labels, working hard to promote its performers in mainstream music circles.

The Folk Music Innovators

While many performers were content to imitate the sounds that they heard, some moved beyond imitation to become innovators. One performer who began his career imitating and analyzing the music of blues performers was a guitarist named John Fahey (1939-   ). Fahey went so far as to take the name Blind Joe Death on his recordings, in homage to early blues singers with names like Blind Lemon Jefferson. Although Fahey's name came

The New Lost City Ramblers. Back to front: John Cohen (guitar), Mike Seeger (fiddle), Tom Paley (banjo).
PHOTO COURTESY: Flying Fish Records.

from the blues tradition, his guitar playing drew on diverse influences, including the music of Indian sitar players, country-western
music, church hymns, and early jazz. Fahey's records are all instrumental, and often consist of long, rambling solos. He exploits the
many different tonalities that he can draw from the guitar to create
tone poems that express different moods.

The influence of Fahey's self-produced records was profound.
Guitarists were no longer limited to playing accompaniments for
songs. They could explore the entire range of possibilities that the
instrument offered. Fahey spawned a generation of players in a
category that has taken the name "new acoustic music." Drawing
on folk traditions, the new acoustic musicians meld different styles
from around the world to create new sounds and styles. The new
acoustic style embraces everyone from Fahey and his followers like
Leo Kottke, to David Grissman (1945-   ), a mandolin-playing
composer who works in bluegrass, jazz, and swing styles, to pianist
George Winston, originally a Fahey-style guitarist who now paints
his tone pictures on the piano.

The British Folk Music Revival

The revival of interest in folk music in America did not go un-
noticed in Britain. Dixieland jazz had been popular in England
since the late 1940s, along with American big-band music that
had been imported to England during the Second World War. In
the late 1950s, British bands began to imitate American groups
like the Weavers, mixing in the influences of American jazz and
pop music. The new form of music was called "skiffle"; Lonnie
Donegan, one of the creators of this style, had a hit with Leadbelly's
prison song, "The Rock Island Line."

Two English folksingers reacted against skiffle, because they felt
English singers should be reviving English music, not imitating
American pop forms. They were A.L. (Bert) Lloyd, a scholar
performer who sang in a high tenor voice, and Ewan MacColl
(1915-   ), a singer/songwriter who went on to compose the
popular love song, "The First Time Ever I Saw Your Face." The
two formed the Singer's Club in London in order to encourage
young musicians to play British folk music.

In the 1960s, several popular groups and solo performers met
the challenge of MacColl and Lloyd to perform their own music.
The Ian Campbell Folk Group absorbed the influence of American
songwriters and instrumentation (guitar-banjo-bass), taking a modern approach to British folk and contemporary songs. The Water-

sons, a family group from Yorkshire, revived the art of British harmony singing; they in turn influenced other revivalists to sing in an unaccompanied style, such as the influential group the Young Tradition. Martin Carthy began his career in a London-based group singing topical songs, but soon turned to performing traditional ballads and songs with a unique, percussive guitar accompaniment.

The English folk boom really blossomed through the '70s and '80s. Groups and solo singers moved away from the standard songs and ballads that had been the staple of the revival. They turned to less-known collections, older singers, and early recordings to revive the many special regional musics heard throughout the British Isles.

In Ireland, Paddy Maloney formed the Chieftains to perform Irish dance music in a highly arranged and entertaining style. Early on in the folk revival, the Clancy Brothers of Ireland performed Irish songs with banjo or guitar accompaniments that showed the influence of the Weavers and other American folk bands; later, Irish bands would perform in a more traditional style. In the 1970s, many young Irish musicians formed bands that showed the influence of jazz, rock, and other popular musics. Planxty was the first band to feature a high-energy, rhythmic accompaniment to Irish tradi-

Joan Baez, c. 1964.
PHOTO COURTESY: Vanguard Records.

tional music that was derived from popular rock bands. De Danaan and the Bothy Band followed with their own personal blends of traditional and popular music.

Similar revivals of regional music occurred throughout the British Isles. The Boys of the Lough is a popular band that combines the fiddle music of the Shetland Islands (North of Scotland) with Irish and Northumbrian (Northern England) song and dance. In Scotland, the School of Scottish Studies was formed to serve as an archive and clearinghouse for Scottish music. Scottish bands Silly Wizard and the Battlefield Band both take a modern approach to reinterpreting the traditional music of that country.

R·E·A·D

DeTurk, David A. and A. Poulin, Jr., eds., *The American Folk Scene*. New York: Dell/Laurel, 1967.

Dylan, Bob, *Lyrics, 1962-1985*. New York: Knopf, 1985.

Guthrie, Woody, *American Folksong*. New York: Oak Publications, 1961.

Guthrie, Woody, *Bound for Glory*. New York: E. P. Dutton, 1968.

Klein, Joe, *Woody Guthrie: A Life*. New York: Knopf, 1980.

Lomax, John, *Adventures of a Ballad Hunter*. New York: Macmillan, 1947.

Lomax, John and Alan, *Negro Folk Songs as Sung by Leadbelly*. New York: Macmillan, 1936.

Sandberg, Larry and Dick Weissman, *The Folk Music Sourcebook*. New York: Knopf, 1976.

Scaduto, Anthony, *Dylan*. New York: Grosset & Dunlap, 1971.

Seeger, Pete, ed. by Jo M. Schwartz, *The Incompleat Folksinger*. New York: Simon & Schuster, 1972.

L·I·S·T·E·N

Almanac Singers, *Talking Union*. Folkways 5285

Anderson, Eric, *The Best of*. Vasnguard VSD 7/8.

Baez, Joan. Vanguard 2077

Blake, Norman, *Old and New*. Flying Fish 010

Bok, Gordon. Folk Legacy 40

Bothy Band, *Best Of*. Green Linnet 3001

Boys of the Lough. Shanachie 79002

Byrds, *Sweetheart of the Rodeo*. Columbia 9670

Carlin, Bob, *Fiddle Tunes for Clawhammer Banjo*. Rounder 0132

Carthy, Martin. Topic 340

Carthy, Martin, *Crown of Horn*. Rounder 3019

Chieftains, *1*. Claddagh CC2

Chieftains, *5*. Shanachie 79025

Clancy Brothers and Tommy Makem, *Rising of the Moon*. Tradition 1006
Clannad, *2*. Shanachie 79007
Collins, Shirley and the Albion Country Band, *No Roses*. Crest 11
Cooney, Michael. Folk Legacy 35.
Dalglish, Malcolm and Grey Larsen, *Banish Misfortune*. June Appal 016
De Danann, *Selected Jigs, Reels and Songs*. Shanachie 79001
Dylan, Bob, *Biograph*. Columbia C5X 38830
Fairport Convention, *Liege & Lief*. A & M 4257
Fiddle Fever, Flying Fish 247
Fuzzy Mountain String Band, *Summer Oaks and Porch*. Rounder 0035
Glazer, Joe, *Labor Songs*. Collector 1918
Grissman, David, *Early Dawg*. Sugar Hill 3713
Grissman, David, *The David Grissman Quintet*. Kaleidoscope F-5
Guthrie, Arlo. Reprise 2141.
Guthrie, Woody, *Dust Bowl Ballads*. Folkways 5212
Guthrie, Woody, *Sings Folk Songs*. Folkways 2483-84
Guthrie, Woody, *Songs to Grow On*. Folkways 7015, 7020
Hartford, John, *Catalog*. Flying Fish 259
Hartford, John, *Mark Twang*. Flying Fish 020
Highwoods Stringband, *Fire on the Mountain*. Rounder 0023
Lloyd, A. L. Topic 103
Lloyd, A. L. *First Person*. Topic 118
New Lost City Ramblers, *20 Years of Concert Performances*. Flying Fish 102
New Lost City Ramblers, *Vols. 1-5*. Fokways 2395-2399
Newgrass Revival, *Fly through the Country*. Flying Fish 016
Planxty, *The Collection*. Shanachie 79012
Red Clay Ramblers, *Merchant's Lunch*. Flying Fish 055
Seeger, Mike, *Old Time Country Music*. Folkways 2325
Seeger, Mike, *Music from True Vine*. Mercury 1-627.
Seeger, Mike and Peggy Seeger, *Peggy 'n' Mike*. Argo 62.
Seeger, Pete, *America's Favorite Ballads*. Folkways 2320-2323
Seeger, Pete, *Darling Corey*. Folkways 2003
Seeger, Pete, *Songs of Struggle and Protest*. Folkways 5233
Seeger, Pete, *Where Have All the Flowers Gone?* Folkways 31026
Seldom Scene, *Old Train*. Rebel 1536
Silly Wizard, *Caledonia's Hardy Sons*. Shanachie 79015
Spence, Bill and Fennig's Allstars, *Hammered Dulcimer*. Front Hall 01
Steeleye Span, *Please to See the King*. Crest 8
Various, *Berkeley Farms*. Folkways 2436
Various, *Broadside Reunion*. Folkways 5315
Various, *Lonesome Valley*. Folkways 2010
Various, *Melodic Clawhammer Banjo*. Kicking Mule 209
Watersons, *For Pence and Spicy Ale*. Topic 265
Weavers, *Greatest Hits*. Vanguard VSD 15/16.
Weavers, *On Tour*. Vanguard 6537E.

Glossary

accent: An accented note is one that stands out from other notes in a melody. Singers use various techniques to accent a note; see *attack*.

attack: A sudden change in volume or speed in performing a note or notes. A singer or instrumentalist uses attack to *accent* a single note or a melodic phrase.

ballad: A narrative song that tells a story. Compare *epic*; see also *broadside ballad* and *Child ballad*.

bass run: A group of bass notes played on the lower strings of the guitar to form a brief melodic phrase.

bending a note: A technique used by instrumentalists and vocalists to slightly alter a pitch.

bluegrass: A form of country string music pioneered by mandolin player Bill Monroe (1911-   ). The classic bluegrass band consists of mandolin, banjo, guitar, fiddle, and bass.

blues: A form of *lyric song* consisting of short verses centered on feelings of loneliness, trouble in love or life, or protest against living conditions. The *twelve-bar blues* consists of three lines of four bars each; this is the typical rhythmic organization for blues songs. See *country blues* and *urban blues*.

bothy ballad: Songs and ballads sung on Scottish *bothies* (dormitories) where hired workers lived while employed on farms.

broadside ballad: Ballads composed from the years 1500 to 1900, printed on a single sheet of paper, and sold in the streets or at county fairs. See *ballad*; compare *Child ballads*.

breakdown: A general term used to describe Southern dance tunes, usually in $\frac{4}{4}$ time. Compare *reel*.

call and response: A style of group singing in which a leader sings one part of the song (usually the verse) and the entire group follows with another part of the song (usually the *chorus*).

cantaireachd: A system of oral notation used by Scottish musicians to learn the melodies of the traditional bagpipe music, *pibroch*.

ceol mor: Gaelic for the "great music." Used by the Scottish to describe their traditional bagpipe music. See *pibroch*.

Child ballads: Ballads collected by American folklorist Francis James Child (1825-1896); considered to be among the oldest and best narrative songs in the British Isles and America. See *ballad*; compare *broadside ballad*.

chorus: A special phrase, line, or group of lines that is repeated throughout a song at regular intervals.

commonplace: A word or phrase that is used to describe similar situations or individuals in a ballad or song. For example, a good-looking woman will be described as having "cheeks as red as any rose" and "lily-white skin."

compression: A process in *oral transmission* in which the story of a *ballad* is shortened to focus on its most memorable events. See *emotional core*.

continuity: The process through which an individual or an entire culture continues to practice age-old customs, such as the singing of songs that are many centuries old, Compare *variation*; see *folk music*.

contra dance: Traditional British and U.S. social dances performed in two facing lines. Compare *morris dance, Playford dance,* and *step dance.*

country blues: The original blues forms that developed throughout the South. These songs are often accompanied by acoustic guitar.

dip: A sudden drop in pitch from a high note to a lower one. A dip can range from a large and dramatic drop to a very small one.

drone: A constant, unchanging note. On the bagpipes, the drone pipes play a single note, which accompanies the melody. The fifth string on a banjo is sometimes called a drone string because its pitch is rarely changed.

emotional core: The single most important event in a ballad or song; the situation that the ballad story highlights.

epic: A long narrative song that tells the entire life of a hero or heroine in a series of exploits. Compare *ballad.*

falsetto voice: An unnaturally high singing voice used by a singer to perform well above his or her normal range.

field holler: A combination song and shout that was performed by Blacks while they worked in the fields. Field hollers were used by workers to communicate with each other and to pass the time.

floating verse: A verse that moves from song to song, which may or may not be related or linked to the other verses in a song.

formulaic ending: A verse or group of verses used to end a ballad. This grouping will be repeated from song to song.

gapped scale: A scale with some *intervals* that are larger than major or minor seconds. For example, a scale might consist of G–B–D–E–F#; "gaps" fall between G and B (the A is not used) and B and D (the C is note used).

glide: Moving from a low pitch to a higher one in a smooth, unbroken arc.

grace note: A note or notes complementing a primary melody note. See *ornament.*

high, lonesome sound: Describes the intense, nasal singing style of many Southern American singers.

hornpipe: A dance tune performed in ¼ time, at a moderate pace, typically with many dotted notes.

interval: The space between two notes.

intonation: For an instrumentalist, intonation indicates the way in which different notes are played. A violinist with "good intonation" plays each note exactly true to the appropriate scale pitch; "bad intonation" indicates that the pitches are slightly off.

isolation: A culture that is cut-off from all other groups in a particular area is said to be isolated.

isometric: If a single rhythmic pulse is used throughout a piece of music, the rhythm of the piece is said to be isometric.

jig: A dance tune in §, §, or ¹² time.

localization: Changing of place names in a ballad to "localize" the story. Singers in Ohio might incorporate into old songs names of rivers and towns that are known to them, for example. Compare *universalization.*

lyric song: A song that expresses an emotion, rather than tells a story. Compare *ballad.*

morris dance: A traditional English ritual dance. The common morris dance consists of two parallel lines of three men each. The dancers usually wear bells around their ankles and carry either sticks that they clash together at specific points in the dance or handkerchiefs that are twirled above their heads. Compare *contra dance, Playford dance,* and *step dance.*

off-beat: In most music, the rhythmic pulse (or basic beat) is divided into groups of two (duple rhythm) or three (triple rhythm) subpulses. The first beat is usually accented; the others are considered off-beats or weaker pulses. In *syncopation,* the off-beat is accented, upsetting the normal expectation of hearing the primary or first beat accented.

open tuning: A system of tuning a guitar in which the six strings, when unfretted, produce a chord.

oral transmission: The spreading of a song or dance tune from musician to musician through performance, rather than a written score. In other words, musicians learn new songs by hearing other musicians play or sing them.

ornament: Any change that a singer or instrumentalist makes in the performance of a note, including adding *grace notes, bending a note to change its pitch, gliding up to a note, or using vibrato.*

participation: When a cultural group freely mixes with other cultures, it is said to participate in the broader general culture. Compare *isolation.*

pentatonic scale: "Pentatonic" is Greek for five tones; a pentatonic scale consists of five notes, and is the most common folk scale.

pibroch: Short for *piobaireacd,* the Gaelic term for a slow-moving, stately air that is played on the Scottish bagpipes.

Playford dance: A group of dances collected and published by John Playford (1623-1687) popular in 17th and 18th century England.

playparty: A short song performed primarily for amusement, among children or young adults. Consisting of three or four *floating verses* taken from other popular songs.

protest song: A song expressing discontent with living conditions or addressing a specific social problem.

reel: A dance tune in $\frac{4}{4}$ time played at a fairly rapid pace.

ring shout: A religious song performed by a group of singers while dancing in a circular or ring formation. The vocal style combines singing, chanting, and shouting.

selection: The process through which a culture chooses the songs or dance tunes that it will perform. See *oral transmission.*

shape-note hymns: A group of hymns taught by singing masters in the 18th and 19th centuries by using specially printed hymn books that featured different shaped notes. Each shape (a diamond, a triangle, a square, and so on) corresponded to a different pitch. By reading the shapes, a singer who could not read ordinary music notation could know which pitch to sing.

spiritual: A general term given to hymns performed by Black singers that deal with topics of special interest to them, particularly the promise of freedom in heaven. Spirituals are performed in the half-shouting, intense vocal style of all Black religious music.

step dance: Dances that involve complex foot and lower-leg movements.

strathspey: A dance form from Scotland that is in $\frac{4}{4}$ time, featuring many "Scot's snaps," a sixteenth note followed by a dotted eighth. This feature gives the music a jagged sound.

string band: A group of stringed instruments, often fiddle, banjo, and guitar, played together to perform Southern dance music.

strophe: The standard organization of all European folk songs into stanzas or groups of two or more melodic lines that are repeated throughout a song. Each time the melody is repeated, new words can be fitted to it.

syncopation: Changing the basic *accent* in a piece of music in order to emphasize the *off-beat.* Syncopation is fairly common in African music, and was one of the key elements to be introduced into American folk styles by Black musicians.

universalization: The elimination of references in songs to specific place names. Compare *localization.*

urban blues: A form of blues that emerged in the post–World War II years, particularly in Chicago. Performed by small groups usually consisting of electric guitar, piano, bass, harmonica, and drums.

variant: Songs that tell similar stories but have either different words or melodies are called variants.

variation: Changes in melody or words made by individual singers. See *oral transmission.*

vibrato: A rapid quavering of the voice slightly above and below the melody note.

wassail: Literally means "good health." A song traditionally sung to bring good luck or health to a household.

waulking songs: Songs sung by Scottish women while they "waulk" or stamp out newly woven cloth.

worksong: Songs that are sung to help a group of workers perform more efficiently by keeping all hands working at the same time and at the same speed.

Index